P9-BYW-706

GET UP
OR GIVE UP

GET UP
OR GIVE UP

How I Almost Gave Up On Teaching

MICHAEL BONNER

A POST HILL PRESS BOOK

Get Up or Give Up:
How I Almost Gave Up On Teaching
© 2017 by Michael Bonner
All Rights Reserved

ISBN: 978-1-68261-587-4
ISBN (eBook): 978-1-68261-588-1

Cover Photography by Paris Silver, Parisphoto.com
Cover Design by Tricia Principe, triciaprincipedesign.com
Interior Design and Composition by Greg Johnson/Textbook Perfect

No part of this book may be reproduced, stored in a retrieval system, or transmitted by any means without the written permission of the author and publisher.

Post Hill Press
New York • Nashville
posthillpress.com

Published in the United States of America

To my amazing parents, Michael and Freda Bonner.
Your love and support through my darkest hours
has propelled me to be a man who continues to persevere.
I wish I could give you the world and more.
One day, I will be able to fully show you how much you mean to me.
This is just the beginning.
....

To my siblings Andrae, Vonda, Kelly Jr., Candace, and Khaliah.
I love you all with my entire being.
You have never shown a millimeter of jealousy or envy.
Instead you have shown kilometers of love and support and
I am honored to call you family.
....

To Jonathan and Chelsea Jackson, Carnella Alston,
Ashley Hunt, and Amani Henry, you all are the epitome
of what true friendship should be.
Please know you will always have my support
as we continue through this journey of life.
Your love and support is the reason this book could be birthed.
....

Ron Clark and Kim Bearden—you two are like
the aunt and uncle that everybody wants to have the sleepover with
because you are so amazing and transparent.
Thank you for providing your wisdom and support
in a world that can be full of jealousy.
....

Last but not least, to Ellen DeGeneres.
Thank you for allowing your love for educators
to fuel me to greater heights and create a new level of possibilities
for my students. You will always have my support.
....

Contents

Foreword

One day I was speaking at a high school. Before I spoke, I was talking with the principal when a student walked by. They exchanged pleasantries and he went on to class. As soon as he turned the corner, the principal said proudly: "You know, he's gonna make a great prisoner one day." Like you, my jaw dropped because I knew that solely left to her leadership, this child would have no chance to succeed. As an educator in the field of culturally relevant instruction and implicit bias, I know that students will rise or recede to the levels of expectations set for them. I left that school nervous for the future, not just for that child, but many of the students across the country suffering from what former President George W. Bush referred to as the "soft bigotry of low expectations." Then I turned on *The Ellen DeGeneres Show* and saw Michael Bonner.

I know that I did not physically weep when I saw Michael's story but I wept inside. I wept because I kept saying to myself that *this* is what every child needs! Give a child hope and he will give you his heart. Give a child a challenge and she will fight to prove she is capable to conquer it. Show children that if they work hard that they can indeed have a stake in the American dream *regardless* of their circumstances and they will work harder than we could ever expect for a better future. Michael understands this, and *Get Up or Give Up* is his testimonial to this fact.

My hope is that everyone reads this book because it is not just the journey of the teacher but the journey of the student. It is not just about Michael's journey to *The Ellen DeGeneres Show* but his journey to becoming a teacher who sees himself in every student who enters his classroom. He therefore knows that if he does not get up for them every morning, *they* might give up and that is unacceptable for Michael. My hope is that in reading this book, you will realize that it is unacceptable for *any* of us to give up on our children, inside *or* outside of the classroom.

Yours in service,
Dr. Omékongo Dibinga
Director, UPstander International

Introduction

The *Ellen DeGeneres Show* had not been a TV show I watched—but that all changed in October 2016 when I received the call of a lifetime. Seems that someone from the show had caught wind of my latest experiment in teaching, a music video that I created as a reward for my students passing a summative reading assessment. During this time, the majority of my students were not grasping the material I was teaching. From their scores, I knew if I did not change my method of instruction or find a way to reach them, I could possibly ruin their chances of understanding more complex text later in the year.

Thus began the adventure of a lifetime for my students and me as we whisked our way to Los Angeles, to be celebrated for innovation in teaching and learning—and to a whole different orbit for my babies from one of the poverty-stricken areas in northeastern North Carolina.

My journey to *The Ellen DeGeneres Show* undoubtedly would have been the last thing on my mind when I grew up in North Carolina. What I envisioned for myself were regular appearances on TV as a professional basketball player in the NBA, counting thousands of dollars, and living comfortably in a mansion some-where in a large city, a dream that many young men embark on in order to quickly change their lives and the lives of those around them. That dream carried me through high school and into college, but circumstances—and yes, maybe being a little short on the required talent—changed the trajectory of my career path.

As a student who gave a teacher or two a rough time, never did I dream that the field of education would be my landing spot. It never occurred to me that I would make an impact on the lives of so many children. That I would have the opportunity to speak at national conferences, create a new culture of positivity at South Greenville Elementary, or be a guest on *The Ellen DeGeneres Show*—twice.

But thanks to the power of thinking differently and not accepting the status quo in education, I was blessed to be able to surmount many obstacles on the way to a rewarding career in teaching—that I almost *gave up on*. That is the story I want to share with you. One that is full of truth and honesty. A journey of a lifetime.... And it all started in a tiny area of northeastern North Carolina.

1

The "Trap"

"Injustice anywhere is a threat to justice everywhere."
–MARTIN LUTHER KING, JR

Perquimans County, North Carolina. This is where life for me began. To some it is called home, but to others it is referred to as the "*Trap.*" It is a county of no more than 14,000 people and from my understanding, it is the only county in the United States of America with a bascule bridge that is literally shaped like the letter "S." Highway 17 runs through this town, which creates only one major intersection. You have one Food Lion, three gas stations, and only four schools for each segment of the K–12 infrastructure. There are only two basketball courts, one tennis court, and no business or club to really generate innovative thinking and creative arts for millennials.

The affluent stay in the Albemarle Plantation waterfront golf community, and the word around town is to avoid visiting "New Jack" projects (which was named after the Mario Van Peebles movie *New Jack City*) or King Street for fear of getting robbed.

You will not find any major artists or movie stars stopping through Perquimans nor any new skyscrapers being developed downtown. There is no movie theater, no Walmart, no arcade, nor skating rink. Sounds pretty boring, right? Well a lot of times, it was. I am sure you can imagine how "excited" I was when my parents told me to go outside to play. I quickly learned we had to become creative in order for us to substitute the limited opportunities provided to us at such a young age.

Growing up in a small town also had its perks. Because we did not live in an overcrowded city, family was the core of everything. You could always guarantee a gigantic turnout at sporting events, family reunions, or cookouts at Missing Mill Park. Perquimans is mainly known for baseball due to the sports legend himself, Jim "Catfish" Hunter, a Hall of Fame inductee, but football and basketball were also major sports. To this day, I can still feel the adrenaline fire through my neural connectors when I think about running out of the locker room onto the basketball court before a big game. To see my family members in the stands cheering their hearts out when we played against Edenton, Northeastern, or Plymouth will forever be engrained in my mind. These were the moments where individuals from all walks of life actually united for a common cause. At that moment it was not about where you stayed, the color of your skin, or how much money was in your bank account. When it was time for the referee to toss the basketball in the air, the people of Perquimans were only focused on one goal—getting the win. But when the sporting events were over, people returned to their everyday lives. The camaraderie that you saw displayed at the football games after Justin Roberson threw a touchdown pass or when Donald Stepney led the 2003 basketball team to the state championship sort of disappeared. As I saw this dichotomous behavior while I was growing up, I noticed that the same behavior slowly permeated the school system.

I can remember to this day almost every teacher that I had, from my fifth-grade teacher Virginia Jones, who continued to pour into me years after I left her class, to my sixth-grade teacher Nina Felton, who showed me how much I could apply myself. And I cannot forget Mrs. Newby, who was my first-grade teacher. She had the best pedagogy and classroom management known to mankind! It didn't matter if you were Caucasian, African-American, or Hispanic, you could count on having a great time in Mrs. Newby's class and building great friendships. At the age of six, we did not pay attention to the racial constructs that were around us unless somebody of age brought it to our attention. My circle of friends at that point was full of individuals from very different cultural backgrounds, socioeconomic statuses, and ethnicities. But when we entered Mrs. Newby's class, all the differences went out the door. She established a classroom culture of educational rigor inclusive of the differences.

One day I decided to test her classroom management skills by not staying on task in reading. I was talking out loud, being unnecessarily disruptive, and, to be completely honest, I was approaching my education as a joke. This did not turn out in my favor when she decided to contact my mother and father, who were hardworking individuals. I can remember her writing a note to my mother because I was tearing the classroom up. I was instructed to take it to my mother, who was a teacher assistant in kindergarten at the time. Being my mischievous self, I threw the note into the school's central air and heating system and walked back to class trying to fix my facial expressions to match that of a person who had just gotten in trouble. At six years old, I did not think about the invisible force of the wind that would cause the note to be blown among the fans and onto the ground, and which somehow mysteriously made its way into my mother's hand. The "talk" that I received from my father and mother that day after school still keeps me in check when it comes to following the rules and making sure I am a model citizen.

I enjoyed the feeling and understanding of equality that radiated in Mrs. Newby's classroom. But I would soon find out that the classroom culture I had become accustomed to was not a direct reflection of the world.

As I transitioned from elementary school to middle school, I noticed my classroom structure changing and the friends that I made from kindergarten to fifth grade began to shift. We all were excited about going to a different school and having new experiences, but I did not expect our circles to slowly change. The thought of diversity was known, but it was not always established or effectively modeled as we transitioned through human development in our small town. As I was promoted through each grade, I began to watch friends who were dear to me shift from a heterogeneous mixture to a homogenous pool of family members and mutual friends of the same ethnicity. By the time I was in eighth grade, at lunch you could slowly see small pockets of inclusion among different races, but it was becoming a rarity. You can imagine that as we transitioned to high school, the gap of inclusion amongst our social circles narrowed. This was something that I don't think intentionally happened, but this reaction began to affect us in how we communicated and saw the world around us. How we approached political issues or everyday decisions was now influenced from one perspective instead of having the daily privilege of being exposed to different viewpoints through contextual conversations. It was as if we were naturally segregating ourselves, and people would only whisper about it at barbershops or in closed-door conversations. The individuals who drove the older model Crown Victorias with 20-inch rims would park on one side and the individuals who drove trucks with the loud exhaust pipes would park on the opposite side.

One of the rare tangents of common ground that brought us together as a people were sports, specifically basketball and football. When my parents used to tell me to go outside and play, we would go to the library and play basketball on the monkey bars. That is all we had at the time. But when the city decided to build its first concrete basketball court, the excitement transferred like an electrical current among everybody. The first basketball court was built beside Missing Mill park right across the street from the place that serves the best fried chicken in the world, Little Mint—"Home of the Big Fellow"—near a rural area and the library. This court was unique because it was half the size of a full regulation basketball court, but we did not care. We were simply excited to play on concrete instead of a dirt court or monkey bars. This was a place to finally give fuel to our "hoop dreams" that could help us make it out of town.

This court did not have any street lights or painted regulation lines, so city officials would come to lock the basketball court at sunset to prevent anything illegal from happening. But problems quickly arose because the basketball court was too small for the number of individuals who came. People were not used to new infrastructure being built, so the first couple of months individuals were there to enjoy the newness of this project. It was crowded and a solution had to be found to prevent any chaotic situations. So the county decided to build another basketball court, on King Street, which is closer to Section 8 housing and where most of the individuals who played basketball lived. This court would be full regulation size, but the problem was the neighborhood was synonymous with crime. Even though there were some individuals there who were working hard to create a better life for their children, often those negative stereotypes were attached to the entire neighborhood due to the bad choices of some individuals.

Regardless of where the basketball court was being built, as young active children, we were still excited about having somewhere to actually practice and hone our skills. Other counties had AAU teams and gyms to play in, so we were grateful for whatever was given to us. But this basketball court also closed at night due to the lack of streetlights to illuminate the court during game play.

While the basketball court was being built on King Street, the county decided to build a tennis court beside the first basketball court near Missing Mill Park. The tennis court was paved with green paint and the white lines typical of tennis courts, something that the two basketball courts did not have. The tennis court also was kept open until 10 o'clock at night because it was surrounded with six to eight, huge, 25-foot light poles that illuminated the area. This caused a gigantic problem among my peers.

Why? Because Perquimans County was known for baseball, basketball, and football. So when the county decided to invest its financial monies into a new tennis court with beautiful paint and lights, but neglected the two basketball courts that were close by, the disconnect prevented our community from coming together as one. Most importantly, the biggest shocker is that Perquimans did not at that time, and *still does not to this day*, have an official tennis team. What it symbolically represented to us was that we would not be able to get out of the *"Trap."* Why would a group of people take the financial liberty to invest in a sport that most of our athletes did not play as a means to draw attention from recruiters to pay for college? This form of classical conditioning would not stop there but became more aggressive as we transitioned through high school.

In high school, I was aware that it was important for me to start off my freshman year on a good note. Trying to remember my locker combination while the pretty upperclassmen walked by was a hard task. I can remember practically begging my father and mother for money in every clothing store because I wanted to make the best impression amongst this new circle of peers. But as I transitioned through high school, outside the realm of sports, I noticed the social circles around me still changing. It was the typical situation — athletes hung with athletes, scholars ate with other scholars — but there was an even stronger correlation in that observation. Those particular friend circles were racially homogenous. To some, that was okay. The same continuous system and reality did not bother them because it was a way of life. But realistically speaking, having those types of marginalization's in the classroom and around you not only

7

can hinder academic growth, but also not give a true representation of the world that existed outside the county lines. Some teachers recognized this dysfunctional pattern that poisoned our learning experience, but chose to ignore it. Other amazing teachers chose to confront it head-on. That is what happened when I entered Mrs. Dunbar's class my senior year.

Jeanie Dunbar, my high school English teacher, was an amazing educator. She was an older, 5-foot-4, evenly built Caucasian woman. But when she opened her mouth to teach, her personality and love for all students instantaneously made it seem as if she were the same height as I was (at 6-foot-5). She embodied what teachers should be and how they should carry themselves. She infused passion and instructional content in a way that created a new love for education within me. Mrs. Dunbar came from out of town, so she was not afraid to speak against systematic inconsistencies, and it was so refreshing. When you entered her classroom it was similar to drinking a cold glass of water on a blistering hot day. Ethnicity and beliefs were respected and not used for division or personal gain. She influenced us to become critical thinkers and analyze how things were around us. She challenged us with rigorous vocabulary that helped us articulate ourselves in debates and conversations efficaciously.

While I was in her classroom, I also was blossoming into a fantastic basketball player. The academic fire she instilled within me leaked over into the athletic realm, which gave me the opportunity to become a dual threat (academically and athletically). Usually in small towns, when an individual plays sports, their main goal is to make it to the professional level. This was and still is a popular narrative for young African-American men.

In most 1A high schools or in smaller counties, the tallest guy would play forward or center. But due to my skill set, I could also play shooting guard, and that gave me the chance to be recruited by various universities. As a senior, I won the Player of the Year award for the surrounding counties, and became the first male in Perquimans County history to be selected to the North Carolina East vs. West basketball game, and I became one of the first to sign a full ride to an NCAA Division I university. My eyes had been set on the National Basketball Association (NBA) since I was a little boy, and the possibility of making it "out" was becoming a reality.

With so much excitement surrounding basketball at the time, the county decided to invest in a new recreation center—finally! A gym that we could play in and escape the scorching heat during the summer was fine with me; I was tired of getting a tan that made me unrecognizable. Elated does not express my emotions appropriately for how pumped I was to finally experience a brand-new gym. This excitement was short-lived when we found out the location of the gym. Somebody decided that the best spot for this gym would not be within the local community, like the two basketball courts and the tennis court, but near the outskirts of the city limits. That meant we could not walk there. We would need access to a car or ride our bikes at least 5 to 10 miles in order to play at this new facility.

That disappointment would rise to an all-time high when we found out that the best times for the gym to be open for basketball was *only* on Tuesdays and Thursdays from 2 to 4 p.m. We were in school until 2:50 p.m. and by the time we found a ride to the gym, it would be 3:15. Hopefully you'd get to the gym in time to be called on for the next game, but if not, you would have to sit until 3:30 to 3:45. Unfortunately by that time, the pickup games would be sloppy and most individuals were ready to go home. The million-dollar recreation center that was built to serve everybody within the community did not, unfortunately, serve the youth it would most benefit.

I was tired of seeing this pattern repeated, and this did not sit well with my peers either. But Mrs. Dunbar, who was an intellectual, was already ahead of us, providing effective solutions.

During this time, she was reinforcing her conversations about going to college and the importance of earning a college degree. She visually showed us the difference in earnings between a high school dropout versus somebody who has earned a four-year degree. With that type of educational conversation going on in the classroom, I decided to go the school office to check out scholarships. At that time, I had scholarship offers from two stunning Division I Historically Black colleges. Those were Winston-Salem State University and South Carolina State University. Even though I had received an athletic scholarship for a full ride in basketball, the purpose of my office visit was to create an educational awareness for myself and my friends who were not in the same position as me athletically.

As we walked down the dimly lit corridor near the library into the front office, there were two sheets of paper on the wall. These were the only two scholarships posted at the time. One was from the local Rotary Club for $500 and the other was a Jim "Catfish" Hunter scholarship, which was also worth $500. The requirements were set to a certain GPA and from my memory, you had to write an essay on why you deserved the scholarship.

Because I already had scholarship offers on the table and I was unaware that you can have multiple scholarships, I skipped right past those and continued through my day. From that point on, I never gave much thought as to why there were only two scholarships posted because I thought that was normal.

The next year, after I went off to play basketball for Winston-Salem State University, my mother became the guidance counselor at Perquimans County High School. A trip back home to see my family was vital because I knew she and my father had missed me tremendously. Winston-Salem State University was four hours away, so the distance made the reunion even sweeter. As I visited her office, she was so excited. She showed me a poster of me she had printed out and allowed me to tour the school to see how they'd converted the old gym into a library. Then I followed her to the supply room. She was looking for some manila folders to file some documents, but my eyes gravitated towards this huge silver filing cabinet that was near the door. I calmly said to her, "Mom, what is this?" She continued to search for her items with her head down and said, "Those are all the scholarships that we have for seniors who are about to apply and enroll for college." I stood there dumbfounded for a moment with a cold stare and look of disbelief on my face. As she heard the awkward silence, she looked up and saw my expression; she could tell I did not believe her. She then proceeded to pull out each row in the filing cabinet, showing me a plethora of scholarships. Scholarships I had not known existed, like financial awards for individuals who were left-handed.

I remember how I felt at that moment. Cold, numb, and indifferent. It felt as if somebody had laid an 18-wheeler truck on my heart and refused to pick it up. In that moment, I realized my friends who were stuck back at home or working in dead-end jobs had never really been exposed to the tools that could have freed them from the *"Trap."* I felt disappointment because I was led to believe that my classmates, friends, and family members did not want to better their education, but reality showed that somebody had dropped the ball in informing them about the numerous programs that exist to help individuals from Title I schools—which receive funding from the government due to the number of children from low-income families—and from poverty-stricken areas to succeed.

In that pivotal moment, everything came into focus. I emotionally and mentally could not handle the clear picture of the systematic injustice in which I grew up. The thought of it actually began to irritate me and forced me to start thinking about how I could help others. I went on to have conversations with classmates who were still living in Perquimans County on what we could do to create better opportunities academically. The one conversation that stuck out the most was with a distant family member, whom I can clearly remember stating,

> "I am so proud of you, Mike. You were blessed to able to get out and make something of yourself, but I am stuck at a crossroad. I want to stop the illegal activity I am doing so I can provide for my family the right way. But if I work at the McDonald's for $7.25 an hour, I will not be making real money. I make $2,000-$3,000 per month selling drugs, and going to work a legal job making only $1,000 a month will not get the bills paid. I feel like I am trapped."

For some who might have grown up in a metropolis type of city you may not be aware of this, but there are certain barriers you encounter when you grow up in a small town. You essentially only have two options or pathways to make it out of that town in order to create a better opportunity for yourself and your family. Those two choices are either academics or athletics. The first pathway can be to excel academically: Your family is knowledgeable about the process of taking the SAT/ACT, they have stayed on top of your degree completion plan while also making sure you took extra credit college courses, and have pulled information about scholarships since you were a freshman. Or, you could take the route that I took, which was athletics. You could have pretty good grades, but in the sports arena, you dominated every individual who dared to cross your path.

This dichotomous ideology can be traced throughout history in many cultures, but we ignore the fact there is a large cluster of individuals who are not gifted athletically, do not have the academic firepower, or adequate support at home. These individuals are more than likely to get *"trapped"* because they are not exposed properly to the tools that are available for students to have a chance to break the cycle that many generations fall into. They may not have the parental support at home to make sure that they are sticking to their academic studies or they may not have access to the proper equipment, state-of-the-art gyms, and well-funded AAU teams that will help them receive a collegiate sports scholarship.

Having so many friends that fell into that group of individuals is what caused my initial reaction to my phenomenal mother showing me more than 100-plus scholarships. To read about educational injustice is one thing, but to escape the grasp of this monster and see your friends die by its hands is not a comforting feeling. In that eye-opening moment of truth, I knew something had to change. Seeing my friends and family put at a disadvantage through multiple circumstances, from academics to the athletic arena, did not sit well with me. A feeling of disgust built within me towards the mistreatment of individuals everywhere. Each experience I had growing up from kindergarten to twelfth grade began to work itself back into my memory and created a vivid picture about how the world can potentially work.

Practicing at night when I could not see on a basketball court to perfect my jump shot, only to glance 20 yards away to see an empty tennis court with its lights on staring back at me, created feelings of not being valued. Remembering that moment of seeing the large number of scholarships that I was not aware of in my senior year stare back at me, ignited a motivation to create change. It was at that moment that my indignation and the desire to see educational equity be enforced came over me, and I decided to do something about it. I was going to fight as hard as I could to make it to the NBA and use the money to invest back into my city. But in the meantime, as I rode back to Winston-Salem, I knew there was only one way for me to solve this problem, and that was for me to get out of the *"Trap"* and find a way to free others.

2

One Million— $100,000—$30,000

"Your work is going to fill a large part of your life,
and the only way to be truly satisfied
is to do what you believe is great work.
And the only way to do great work
is to love what you do."
–STEVE JOBS

When I arrived at Winston-Salem State University as a freshman, I was completely awestruck. The drive seemed like I was traveling across the United States from Perquimans County to "The City of the Arts and Innovation." When I graduated from high school, I enrolled as a college student for summer school. This was a chance for me and my roommates to get acclimated to the college atmosphere and lifestyle and together play in the North Carolina East vs. West basketball game. It was a swift transition for me and my family, but was beneficial for me to become acclimated to a city of this size. I can remember many nights staring from my dorm in Rams Commons, amazed by the skyscrapers outlined in the night sky. I fell in love with how accessible everything was. This adventure helped crush the "small town mentality" that was so easily reinforced within my head.

Despite the temptation to stay home and go to a local university, accepting this scholarship allowed me to create a new world for myself. I knew the experiences I would receive, the people I would meet, and the knowledge I would gain would allow me to become more dynamic in my efforts to help those back home. This step of faith would solidify the necessary components that would help me to grow into a man of character and integrity. Concurrently, this was a chance for me to go off and prove myself to my hometown. Being the first male from Perquimans County to sign to a Division I collegiate scholarship was an enormous feat. In fact, it was unheard of. Most individuals who went off to college for the athletics eventually ended up dropping out and returning home. I wanted to make sure I didn't disappoint those who'd poured so much time and energy into my journey. The thought of the countless supporters, long drives to AAU trips, and financial sacrifices my family made constantly weighed on me. To disappoint them was not an option.

I found myself enjoying the college life more than I'd expected. My high school graduating class was around 115 people, but my freshman class at college was estimated to be at least five times that size in 2008. The exhilarating feeling I received as I walked around on campus is something I cannot necessarily put into words. Fried Chicken Wednesdays and the social gatherings on the yard between classes were some of the best moments to me. The instructors made learning new material fun. The boy to girl ratio was in favor of me as I gazed at the beautiful young women who attended this university, and there were no complaints from my teammates either. Choosing to go to a HBCU (Historically Black Colleges and Universities) was one of the best decisions I have ever made. To see different individuals from different cities and ethnicities join together for the common goal of achieving academic excellence was something that deserves to be highlighted. I decided to major in psychology because I knew that I would make at least six figures when I finally received my bachelor's degree—I did not pick a major that I was passionate about because my brain was so wrapped around fulfilling my hoop dreams. Besides, I knew if I could not make $1 million, the fallback plan of being a clinical psychologist would allow my family and I to live comfortably.

Transitioning to college became increasingly difficult once basketball season began to kick in. I experienced a real wake-up call because the workout regimen and talent at the Division I level was higher than I'd anticipated. While others were enjoying the late-night parties and day-party socializations that are often common on most campuses, we on the team were waking up at 5 a.m. to run 2 to 3 miles and lift weights. From there we would go to 8 a.m. class, where I constantly got in trouble for falling asleep. We would go to lunch and then practice at the end of the day for about 2 ½ hours. I would not get back into my dorm room until 8 o'clock at night. This was my life for the majority of both semesters. I still chuckle to this day because one time, none of the freshmen woke up for a 5 a.m. practice. The upperclassmen were livid when the coaches moved conditioning practice to the afternoon. That did not go well. But that was one of the woes of transitioning to college, experiencing a new culture, and stepping out on something new that nobody has attempted to do.

The early-morning conditioning sessions and late-night practices were all in preparation for our season. And after stepping on the court for the first time in a game at Georgia Tech, I quickly found out what it *really* meant to be a college athlete. There is a gigantic difference from playing against a local school down the street and then having to go against Iman Shumpert (who currently plays for the Cleveland Cavaliers). The crowd at my high school games were, at most, 350 people. But that night at Georgia Tech, the crowd numbered easily over 10,000 people and my nerves were through the roof. That night we lost 92–47. I refused to pick up any phone calls to talk to anybody from back home, mainly out of embarrassment. But little did I know, the hurricane of a season that I was about to experience was just beginning.

We went on to face elite major college programs like Wake Forest University, North Carolina State, and Old Dominion, all in a losing effort. By this time, the overwhelming psychological warfare I was experiencing (within myself) was beginning to affect my studies and my performance on the court. I found myself going through the "freshman blues" as I was struggling to climb out of this mental state. Basketball, something that inherently came so easy to me, now had become my biggest obstacle to overcome. In addition, there was a sense of disappointment and frustration slowly moving through my mind. I was lucky enough to make it out of my town, but I never fully comprehended the work and dedication that it would take to be successful once I got out.

Statistically, that season was one of the darkest moments in my life. I ended up averaging 0.9 points (yes, not even a full point). My fear would eventually grow and manifest itself psychologically to the point it paralyzed me as an athlete. The very sport I once loved, I no longer enjoyed playing. But somewhere deep down inside there was still the fight within me to keep pushing. My parents had established my mindset of perseverance early in my childhood. I felt my athletic career was not panning out as I had envisioned as a child when I practiced late at night on King Street. The thought of transferring slowly began to take root within me, and it became a reality in the upcoming months.

Winston-Salem State University was in the beginning stages of being a Division I school, so we had to face some elite major college basketball programs. Because we did not have the appropriate funding like other universities, we often were outsized and outmatched when we played against our opponents. The result was a losing record and low attendance at our home basketball games. Low attendance at these sporting events created a situation where the school was not making enough money. Here's how it works: If a school is not generating enough money, then there will be a loss of scholarships, which won't help the athletic programs when it came to recruiting top athletes.

The university decided the best decision would be for Winston-Salem State University (WSSU) to drop down to Division II and compete within the Central Intercollegiate Athletic Association (CIAA). For some, this decision was exciting news.

The CIAA tournament is an experience of a lifetime. HBCUs would once again be able to compete against one another and bring back the excitement of winning. But for athletes like me who signed a full-ride scholarship in hopes of competing within the highest division, this was confirmation that a transfer would be necessary. For almost a month, I zoned out in practice and within my studies. My brain was working overtime trying to figure out where the best place would be for me to transfer. Due to my lackluster performance on the basketball court at WSSU, it was a challenge to convince Division I coaches that I would be an asset to their teams. Word got back home that I would possibly be transferring and the initial assumption was that I would attend Elizabeth City State University (ECSU), which was about a 15-minute drive from Perquimans County. Although ECSU was another Division II school, it had a rich basketball history. Both the men and women basketball teams had recently been successful throughout the CIAA tournament and their style of play reflected my skill set. Thoughts of becoming another statistic who left—only to return—home haunted me. But I knew that if I did not take a chance at this moment, my basketball career would never be the same. I contacted the head coach at ECSU and made the decision to become a Viking.

Returning home was bittersweet. Winston-Salem is such an amazing city and it touched my heart in so many ways. In the two years that I was there, I was able to meet so many different people who helped change my perspective on life. To experience so many different opportunities and traveling experiences molded my perspective on how different life can be when you take a chance to step out of your comfort zone. But I knew if I wanted at least to have a shot at making it to the NBA, I must continue to press on despite my love for WSSU, even if that meant leaving behind an amazing city and group of friends I cared for deeply.

When I arrived home, my parents welcomed me with open arms. Their support and constant affirmation for me making my decision comforted me, and I was ready to start off this basketball season on the right foot. Little did I know, transferring home would be a catalyst that would turn my life upside down.

When I transferred from Winston-Salem State University to Elizabeth City State University, the only advice that was presented to me to make sure the transition would be smooth was for me to mail off my academic transcripts. I compromised knowing I would be giving up a full-ride scholarship at WSSU. I decided to take my shot and earn my scholarship funds through my performance on the basketball court instead. Because ECSU was a Division II school, full-ride scholarships were reserved for athletes who consistently put the team in a position to win. My past high school performance was enough to allow the coach to give me a chance to make the team, but the points I averaged at WSSU eliminated my chances of being rewarded with financial assistance. Giving up my full ride for financial aid assistance was a sacrifice. Not having my tuition fully covered any longer meant that I would have to be willing to accept student loan payments after I graduated. But sometimes certain situations in life are a calculated risk. Even though ECSU did not have the same exhilarating downtown life as Winston-Salem, the campus life was still an overall great experience. My teammates welcomed me with opened arms and things were looking promising. Since

Perquimans County is next door, being home and attending church with family members and enjoying the luxurious choice of deciding whether to have the café food or a home-cooked meal was something I quickly grew accustomed to.

When the first game for the season approached, I remember the excitement that oozed from the crowd. It was my very first game back home and so many people came out to support the team. It felt like high school all over again as I ran onto the court with fellow classmates and family members cheering at the top of their lungs. The smiles on my parents' faces was priceless as I could tell they were proud to be experiencing this moment with me. They had endured this struggle by my side and finally were getting a sense of relief. This was my chance to shake off my embarrassing season at Winston-Salem State University and to once again show that I could dominate on the basketball court. This was my chance for redemption.

The game started and, sitting on the bench, I cheered for my teammates as if my life depended on it. I am sure I was yelling a little harder to alert the coach I was ready to get in. But as the first half went by, I was never called upon to enter the game. Shocked? Yes, but I knew there was surely a reason he did not substitute me into the game. The second half was coming and I remained hopeful. I purposely chose to stay optimistic about getting a chance to get back on the court in front of my hometown. But as the second half started and time began to go by on the clock, I found myself still sitting on the bench, waiting for my chance to get into the game. The clock reached 2 minutes left, and by this point all the exhilarating cheers I was chanting died down until I was completely silent. We ended the game with a win, but I walked off the court with my head down, refusing to look up into the stands to see the confusion and hurt on the faces of my family and friends.

The next day the coach called me to his office, along with my parents. This was not a normal thing because I knew I had been working hard to do my job, but I figured it would be to discuss my transition and the reason I did not receive any playing time. As the coach began to talk and the conversation transitioned, I remember holding my mother's foot down because she was tapping her foot as anger rose through her body. When a student transfers from another CIAA school, the student must attend summer school classes as they transition. But there was one issue: Nobody alerted me to this rule. There was no written documentation, no verbal communication, nor was any guideline given to me to outline this necessary procedure. Because I was not alerted about this situation, the NCAA and CIAA decided to revoke my collegiate eligibility—meaning I would not able to play in any games for the entire season. As my parents and I gracefully shook my coach's hand and exited his office, at that moment I knew I had fallen out of love with basketball.

I was invited to participate in practices still, but chronic depression had taken over by then. I did not want to hang out with my teammates, show my face around campus, or even drive back home. Word began to spread about me being ineligible and local newspapers began to reach out for stories. Going through a situation privately is one thing, but publicly dealing with something this fragile only complicate a situation. Feelings of embarrassment and anger fueled by injustice towards me put me in a dark place mentally. Here I was back at home, stuck in this place of discontentment and anger after making the choice to transfer in hopes of fulfilling my hoop dreams. A dream that most African-American young men embark upon in order to create a better life for their families. A dream that would have allowed my parents to retire early or pay off their mortgage. A dream in which I had invested countless hours on those basketball courts during sultry summer days and freezing winter nights. A dream that I had to sit and watch metaphorically be flushed down the drain. Not by my own hands, but by the irresponsibility of somebody else.

As you can imagine the motivation to go to class and listen to the teachers was at an all-time low. I have always been a pretty decent student, but it was almost as if I were grieving a death. That was until I enrolled in a behavioral statistics class with Ronald Poulson. Mr. Poulson is a 6-foot-3, muscular-built African-American professor who is brilliant, to say the least. He received his undergraduate degree from Hampton University in psychology, his master's degree from Northwestern University in experimental psychology, and had accumulated numerous accolades in the higher education field. This was a class that dealt with statistics and bell-shaped curves and to some, it would count as torture to sit through it. But now that I think about it, he rarely moved from behind his desk and still found a way to keep the entire class engaged. He literally taught lessons from his seat 80 percent of the time. The way he spoke and crafted his topics was so captivating and full of life that I did not pay attention to his physical movements throughout the classroom. For an hour, he would guide us throughout each lesson and impart practical, life-changing advice that reached into my soul.

Slowly but surely, another amazing educator entered my life at the right time, and his passion for teaching started lifting the burdens of life from my shoulders. He gracefully confronted issues on academic performance for African-American students at HBCUs versus other ethnic subgroups at PWIs (Predominantly White Institutions). His higher order thinking questions created fulfilling discussions and opportunities for us to expound our thoughts upon current issues. Conversations would extend past the normal time frame for class. Before I knew it, my love for learning was driving out my depression, one class at a time.

One day, he assigned a chapter to read in our statistics book and to prepare for a test with our classmates. He had discussed the importance of working together to achieve a common goal and how research had shown that collaborative pairs can be beneficial for community learning. We heard him, but like many in life, we did not apply what we were told. When we arrived the next day, and he asked who really studied for the exam, the numbers were low. He took a deep breath, and just like the volcano from Pompeii, he erupted, obliterating everything in his path. The verbal hurricane he confronted us with that day for an entire hour still sticks with me. Then, just like the eye of the storm in a hurricane, he calmed down with a deep breath and asked a profound question that would change my college trajectory.

"Why are you here?"

We looked around at one another to see who would be brave enough to answer this question, but nobody dared. He began to elaborate on what our purpose for coming to college was. He quickly debunked the status quo of racking up student loans and investing out time day in and day out, only to land below average academically on the grading scale. He reassured us that students at UNC-Chapel Hill were not approaching their academic studies with a lazy mindset, wasting precious time; instead, they were attacking their school work with tenacity to prepare them for their career fields. He insisted that students at Harvard, Yale, and Duke understood that time was of the essence and obtaining the best scores possible would guarantee them a fighting chance when it came to competing against others in job interviews. He ended class with a strategic closed-ended question that would force us all to decide from that day forward about our intentions on our individual education. A question that would challenge our purpose in life and our passion for education.

"If students at the top universities are working daily to capitalize on their future, shouldn't you start approaching class more seriously in order to have a fighting chance?"

As I left class that day, I went to the waterfront in downtown Elizabeth City with a notebook to evaluate myself and my original purpose for attending college. Striving to make it to the NBA was my main goal in order to provide for my family and community. By this time, I knew that making it to the NBA was virtually impossible. But this topic is not addressed frequently among student-athletes, specifically those who play in schools that are not part of elite major programs within the NCAA hierarchy. More than 480,000 student-athletes compete across the United States in collegiate athletics: 18,684 in men's basketball, and only 1.1 percent are projected to make it to the NBA. Only, *1 percent.* But from a general consensus among athletes and my teammates, most individuals were aiming to play professionally, or at least play overseas, even if that meant sacrificing academics to fulfill that dream. Because of this common thought process, some student-athletes would pick a major in which they may have *some* interest, but in reality, only take because the coursework is easy and allows them more time to pursue becoming a professional athlete. Majors such as sports management, interdisciplinary studies, or even psychology were some of the top choices. And can we blame them? The media has done an amazing job of showing us selective examples of success, such as rappers and athletes, as if they are the only successful individuals who have access to consistent capital.

For me, I selected psychology because of the $100,000 average salary I saw reported online and how that would be considered a beautiful payday where I was from. But it was never my real goal to go into any career field because my eyes were set on the NBA. And after realistically evaluating my situation, although Doctor Poulson's class was engaging and exciting, I was tired of writing 20-page APA-formatted papers about mental disorders. To even come close to making a six-figure salary, I would have to return to school to receive my master's degree and more than likely start my own practice. As I began to evaluate my purpose and reflect upon how to bring about true change, I found myself thinking about what I love. What excites me and brings me joy? What is truly my passion?

My mind immediately thought back to the times where my teammates and I would go into elementary schools for community service to work with children. The smiles upon their faces as I walked up to students was always priceless. To them, it was similar to looking up at a human tree, but for me it was staring into the eyes of our future. It was at those moments I knew what I wanted to do. I knew picking the elementary education world would be ideal for me because children's brains are more malleable; I could possibly confront dysfunctional issues before they entered the higher grades. That afternoon after I left the waterfront, I researched the average teacher's salary. When I saw it was $30,500, that was perfectly okay with me. I was only making $400 a month working at a shoe store in the local mall and $1,800 a month after taxes to me seemed like "real money" for a college student. To help me make my decision is the fact that African-American males only represent 2 percent of teachers in the K-12 education system. Last time I checked a 2 percent probability is greater than a 1 percent probability (to make the NBA), so why not take my shot?

(In case you're wondering about my "change of heart," I had to make up my mind if living life was about making money or making an impact. Growing up in a town where you didn't see any lucrative opportunities, *anything* that would create a quick dollar automatically attracted your attention. I was blessed to grow up and never be hungry, but that didn't stop me from knowing we were not the richest people in the community either. Those observations and living circumstances were critical to me initially choosing a career that would be financially lucrative. After recognizing that making it to the NBA would take a miracle, and my desire to be a clinical psychologist was fleeting, reality set in as a college student. I knew I must quickly find a career that had a foundation I loved.)

The next day I broke the news to Mr. Poulson, and even though initially he was sad because I was exiting his program, he still congratulated me on making a firm decision. He emphasized that he was proud of the way I used metacognition to evaluate my purpose in college and reassured me that I would be an amazing educator. He walked me over to the education department, which was about 15 yards away, and helped me switch my major to elementary education. I knew that I could not deal with the high levels of disrespect from middle school students and high school students, so elementary school would be my best fit. I wanted to make an impact as early as I could in a child's life. With advancements in human development, there has been research that indicates the mind of a child is more malleable in the early years opposed to the teenage years. This would also give me an opportunity to make sure every student had the opportunity to have a fighting chance in an education system that is statistically stacked against minorities and students in low socioeconomic brackets, just like Perquimans County. I wanted to make sure every student I encountered would have the chance to succeed while I provided the available resources. Even if their grades or external features did not meet the standard qualifications, I wanted to give them a fighting chance in our society.

This journey would be tough, but I knew it could be done. Due to the amount of coursework I would have to cover and successfully pass, I would be graduating as a fifth-year senior. But what is more important? Pursuing more money in something I could not care less about, or becoming more knowledgeable in a field that helps shape the young leaders of tomorrow? The choice at this point of my life was evident.

Before switching my major, my GPA was a mediocre 2.6. I knew this must change, so I decided to improve my study habits and increase my work ethic. I began averaging a course load of 18 hours per semester just to finish college, but I was enjoying every moment of it. Learning the material was one thing, but having the ability to experience and apply this information throughout my practicums only confirmed that I made the right decision. For almost a year, I went to class from 8 a.m. to 3 p.m., totally engrossed in educational philosophies, head over to a local restaurant for a quick lunch, and then work from 4 to 9 p.m. I know it was a crazy cycle to be in, but this was something that had to be done in order for me to graduate and make something of myself. During this time, I also met a nice young lady who piqued my interest. We all know how the feelings of love and infatuation can hit us and have us swooning over an individual. Things became serious between us—so serious, I decided to propose before entering my spring semester in college. Oh, the things we do when we believe we are in love!

For my last semester of my student teaching, I found myself enrolled in 22 credit hours, engaged to be married, and learning the ins and outs of becoming a classroom teacher. The Praxis would be my next goal to defeat in order to move forward in the education program. (For those not in the teaching profession, the Praxis is a test in North Carolina that teachers must pass in order to receive their teacher's license. A candidate takes Praxis I in order to be initially admitted into the program. But it is imperative that you pass the Praxis II in your respective subject content (elementary, middle grades, and so on) in order to obtain your license.) I took the Praxis II and did not pass the first time. Pressure began to mount but I knew I had to find a way to get through that last semester. The wedding would happen two weeks after graduation, so it was imperative that I pass the Praxis test so I could actually have a job as a husband and provide for my family. Otherwise, I would be married, but jobless.

Within the following weeks, the education department hosted a job fair where recruiters from across the United States came to seek out fresh educators to bring to their respective counties. During my opening interview, recruiters were taking notes vigorously when I spoke, which was good for me. I received a call from Pitt county in North Carolina as they had a job set up for me at an inner-city school. I jumped at the opportunity as I knew this could greatly benefit me. When I arrived for an interview, I saw the neighborhood and the poor condition of the school, but I was motivated to become a teacher. I knew I wanted to teach and I was excited for this chance. The job interview went well and I remember returning home with a smile on my face, excited about the possibility of locking-in a job before graduation. I decided to dig my heels in with the materials I was studying for the Praxis; the second time around, I passed! What a relief!

Within the next couple of days, I received a call-back from South Greenville Elementary School in Greenville, North Carolina, offering me a fifth-grade teacher position. I said yes without hesitation and I was able to secure my first teaching job two months before I graduated. I remember sharing the news with my college advisor and she told me about the things she had heard pertaining to that school. It had a great many students living in poverty, was low-performing, and located in a tough neighborhood where most educators would not dare to drive.

But to be honest, I did not care. I was feeling good about life again. In a couple of months I would graduate with honors, be married, and begin my first year as an educator. Let the show begin.

3

Harry Wong
Did Not Warn Me

"You need to spend time crawling alone through shadows
to truly appreciate what it is to stand in the sun."

—SHAUN HICK

In many ways, South Greenville Elementary reminded me of
my hometown elementary school, Hertford Grammar. You
cross over the railroad tracks and instantly it seems as if you are
in a different world. The choices of good and evil surround you
every single day, and even at a young age you must constantly
make the decision to stay on the right path, or veer from it. The
thought of being able to contribute to society and help young
individuals discover their own power was an exciting feeling.
Some may suggest that teaching at a Title I school would be
easier because I am an African-American man. But that thinking
is false; it's not based on the premise of how life experiences can
be on separate spectrums even if they are from persons in the

same ethnic subgroup. I came from a loving, two-parent house-hold that made sure my basic needs were met every day. But the majority of my friends came from a single-parent home, lived in Section 8 housing, and received government assistance, and there were others who came from a more affluent background where financial resources were never a problem. The amount of melanin in our skin pigmentation was almost identical, but our life experiences landed us in different places across a bell-shaped curve. Despite those differences, was I aware of the different vernacular and behavioral correlations that happened in my classroom because I was in tune with my culture? Of course, I was. But to be transparent with you, that would not matter once I stepped into my classroom. Every individual student is unique in his or her own right, and each student brings a different perspective and life experience to my classroom.

The number of butterflies that a teacher feels before they step into their classroom for the first time probably could not be measured. If we access the best technology from around the world to detect the range of emotions teachers experience before the first day of school, that number still would not quantify the feelings that a beginning teacher feels. Normally, school districts create a system of events to help beginning teachers prepare for their first year. That, in my opinion, is a brilliant idea due to the amount of work that must be done to prepare and maintain a solid work ethic for the school year. You want to get into your classroom to put down the new name tags, check out a student's past academic history, and begin visualizing how you will create an educational euphoria for your students. But too often, beginning teachers are overloaded with information from mentor teachers and administrators, and spend many sleep-less nights due to the amount of time they search Pinterest for classroom ideas. One book that the beginning teacher coordi-nators gave to me and my cohorts was *The First Days of School* by Harry Wong. I was assured by *everybody* that if I read this book, I would be fine and my transition as an educator would be smooth. Of course, I would experience road bumps and the natural ups and downs of an educator (whatever that cliché means), but this book would help me get through those difficult transitions. That week, I grabbed a gigantic-sized pack of sticky notes and began to mark important sections in the book. These ranged from how my classroom seating would be set up to the proper number of procedures to have for my classroom. I made sure I had my lesson plans in order, my parent contact folder correctly filed, and my lesson plans already prepared two weeks in advance.

I thought I was prepared and ready to take on the task of building our future leaders, but little did I know that I was in store for a rude awakening. Students' misplaced anger towards missing fathers who were not in the home, frustration with past teachers who automatically counted them out based upon where they came from, and an inability to embrace someone new in their life would wreak havoc upon me as I began my career at South Greenville Elementary.

April 15, 2016. This will forever be a day etched into my memory as an educator. As I was approaching the end of my third year as a beginning teacher, I was elated that I had made it this far. This would be my second year as grade level chair and I would have the same team returning, which would ensure our chemistry would be stronger to help propel the kids towards educational excellence. It was awards day at South Greenville Elementary and as usual, the kids were excited about the possibility of being called up on stage. The girls came into my classroom in their cute spring dresses and my boys walked in with a confident strut pretending they were "Mr. Bonner." I chuckled at the thought of a seven-year-old trying to imitate how I walk throughout the classroom and hallway. There was one student who came in at 7:35 that morning and by his demeanor, I could tell he did not want to be in school. For the sake of confidentiality, I am going to call him "Mr. Grumpy." Noticing his attitude, I greeted him with a gentle "good morning" and decided to keep my distance in this situation. I did not want to trigger him to react more negatively towards me or his classmates.

Before we lined up to transition to the cafeteria for awards day, I named each child who would be receiving an award. Kids who were receiving awards were beaming with joy, excited to show their parents the result of their hard work they had produced for the semester. Once Mr. Grumpy found out that he was not receiving an award, that was enough to push him over the edge. He erupted with anger, picked up a chair, and hurled it across the classroom at me. I watched as the chair floated across the classroom, seemingly in slow motion. It was the identical reaction I have to watching the character Neo avoid a slow-motion kick in the *Matrix* movie. I stared in disbelief, looked at this seven-year-old in bewilderment, and immediately questioned his actions. He bellowed, "I'm sick and tired of this school and you. I hate you and it is not fair!" Even though I was in disbelief about a chair being hurled at me from somebody who was not taller than 45 inches, for that singular moment, I was able to keep my composure. I calmly asked my teacher assistant to walk my students to the cafeteria. The state of North Carolina had cut funding for teacher assistants, so at that time one teacher assistant was shared among four of us teachers. Luckily, she was there during her scheduled time to assist me in this process. Some of the kids were pretty were scared, but I made sure I gave them a high-five before they left. Unfortunately for some of them, this was what a normal school day was like, sporadic tantrums and random scenes of disrespect from students throughout the school who were no taller than my kneecap.

Once I was able to clear my students out of my room, I asked Mr. Grumpy to calm down because the consequences would not be favorable to his future. Even during my efforts to de-escalate the situation, his anger began to build at a rate faster than I anticipated. With the entire administration team already in the cafeteria for awards day, I knew I would have to attempt to get him to the cafeteria myself. As soon as I reached out to guide him by the hand to the awards ceremony, Mr. Grumpy kicked me in my shin! At that moment, I almost forgot that I was dealing with a child. Never in a million years would I have thought I would be assaulted by someone who was the same height as my knees. I immediately called his mother to make her aware of the situation. With urgency and frustration in her voice, she stated she was on the way. The journey to the office that day is something I will never forget and one that should never happen to an educator. I was physically tired after carrying a kicking, screaming child through the hallway as his mother came to the office to address the situation. As she reprimanded him, physically I was there, but mentally I was zoned out. Not once in my behavioral management classes were we informed how it is possible that some students could become physically aggressive and *enjoy* having a mindset of insubordination.

For some this may seem like a hostile situation that should not be happening inside of a school system, but the reality is that *this happens in a lot* of schools across America. This type of behavior is not limited to the potential of physical altercations that a teacher may encounter, but also, the blatant verbal/non-verbal disrespect educators face across the country, specifically in Title I schools. Through the Title One funds, which help ensure that all children, even from low-income families, meet the challenging state academic standards, schools have the ability to provide different educational opportunities and services to students so they can achieve the same educational success as their counterparts in wealthier school districts. Also, schools are able to make provisions for students who cannot afford to pay for school lunch by offering a free or reduced lunch rate. I believe the Title I funds that schools across America receive are critical to student success, but individuals, policymakers, and citizens of this country often miss a key concept concerning the funding of these programs.

Students who come from low socioeconomic backgrounds normally respond to life circumstances differently than their counterparts who have all their basic needs met. Eric Jensen, in his book *Teaching with Poverty in Mind*, stated that students who experience hardship do not battle with the normal levels of stress that others experience. Students who live with high levels of stress over a prolonged period with little to no control over their current situations experience chronic stress. Chronic stress begins to engrain negative behaviors that eventually turn into habits. When a student attends school, there is a psychological resistance to the procedures and rules that the teacher is trying to establish. At this point, classroom management and student-teacher relationships begin to try to find ways to coexist in the same environment for the 180 days of a school year.

This was the battle I found myself facing every day, constantly trying to research and develop new strategies and techniques that would help relieve me of the World War III atmosphere that was happening within my classroom. To add to my misery, the school administration thought it was necessary to move another student from a neighboring classroom with the same behavior into my room the next day. At that moment, I was frustrated with teaching and the systematic red tape that must be tiptoed around in order to make true change happen. But I was not ready to throw in the towel just yet because deep down inside, I knew there was potential for me to still make a difference despite the chaotic behaviors that seemed increasingly to get worse.

As the months continued I found myself dragging because my personal life began to affect my professional career. My marriage was beginning to fall apart before my eyes. I have learned over the course of the years that every relationship goes through some type of storm, even the good ones. But the category 5 hurricane of a marriage that I was trying to maneuver through, even as I woke up every day to teach, was something I was not prepared for. It is one thing to deal with a personal situation privately, but for a personal situation to leak into a school environment was another battle I had to face. Sometimes, teachers who are not focused on the well-being of their children love to gossip about things that do not pertain to education at all. A powerful combustion of stress happens when you mix personal tribulations with your career, specifically, as an educator. The negative energy from my classroom and my personal life were dangerous for this reason. Every day, we teachers have the power to mold and shape the young minds that come into our classroom. Evidence-based research tells us that the brain has the power to learn new behaviors or constantly reinforce negative actions/thoughts that could be detrimental to the human brain. As educators, we have the power to ignite neurons and synapses to work together in a harmonious melody in order to create the sweet tune of proficiency. But on the flip side as educators, we also have the power to create monsters in our classroom by feeding students instructional content that is full of bigotry, ignorance, and the like.

In our classrooms, we provide students everything we possibly can in order to equip them with all the necessary tools, but simultaneously there is a danger that lies within our purpose. Whatever an individual teacher is experiencing within their personal life will eventually affect the classroom culture. While I was trying to navigate through my marital storm, I felt my natural demeanor change. My students slowly but surely noticed their teacher, who had been full of energy, transition to one whose personality dried up. Within my classroom, I found myself quickly reacting to any miniscule infraction or behavior that my students displayed. If a student forgot their homework, instead of looking for evidence of effort, I would immediately snap at them and find the harshest consequence in order to "teach them a lesson." And for a moment, I lost myself in this storm. As even close friends walked away, I found myself trying to navigate how to balance being an educator and a husband without completely caving in on my life's purpose. I found myself constantly in reflection, looking at other educators and people, wondering what type of battles they were silently fighting while keeping a smile on their face. For the ones I personally knew who were pulling off this amazing feat, I admired their tenacity compared to my inability to muster the internal strength to similarly smile. Despite the circumstances, I still had some fight left inside of me to keep pushing. Quitting my job was not an option and there was a chance that my marriage could still turn around. So, I continued to press on.

Remember the student who was moved into my classroom after Mr. Grumpy attempted to pull a WWE (World Wrestling Entertainment) stunt move on me? Well, we will call her Ms. Sugar. This is not because she was quick to behave when it was time to pass out candy, but her behavior would often be as sweet as sugar—when she chose to behave. The operative word in the previous sentence is "chose." On one particular day, Ms. Sugar was not in the mood to listen or follow instructions. I had one of the best mini-lessons prepared for teaching how to identify and count money, but she was not responding to any of my pep talks or her peers when I asked them to converse in collaborative pairs. Being that Mr. Grumpy had already made my year one to remember, I decided to play the avoidance card with Ms. Sugar and gather the troops of Bonnerville into their guided reading stations.

Despite my attempts to properly utilize the de-escalation tactics that were acquired through one of my professional development courses, Ms. Sugar was determined not to move and remained seated. Being that she was still at a kindergarten reading level in second grade, I thought it would be helpful to prompt her again. She glared at me as if I had just insulted three generations of her family and screamed, "Didn't I say NO!" Now for some, you may be okay with a child who is about 40 inches tall and weighing seventy pounds to disrespect you. But when I was growing up, something called "respect" was preached and constantly reinforced. I decided to call her mother, but both contact phones were off. Ms. Sugar had four or five other siblings at the school so the thought that her parents could not be reached in case of an emergency often dumbfounded me.

As I was hanging up the phone, Ms. Sugar sank into a deeper level of irritation and started to pick small fights with one of her classmates. As I evaluated the situation, I saw her pick up a library book and toss it like a fastball. Luckily, she struck out by missing a student's head by centimeters. She continued to throw multiple books in the direction of her classmates. For the safety of the students, I decided to restrain her with a snug hug and bring order back to my classroom. Ms. Sugar swung, kicked, and even decided to bite me so I would let go of her, but the amount of damage she could do to the other students around her could not be ignored. All teachers in our classrooms had walkie-talkies for emergency situations, so I directed my student teacher assistant to throw the walkie-talkie to me so I could radio the school administration for help. For almost five minutes, I sat holding a child who was kicking and screaming while waiting for the proper help to arrive and simultaneously trying to make sure my guided reading groups transitioned smoothly to their stations.

After Ms. Sugar was removed from my classroom, once again I sat there in complete silence. My students were still moving throughout the room, but who in the world wants to teach after being assaulted by a student? Not this guy. These types of situations were becoming too frequent. Not only within my classroom, but inside my school. Just like a sanitation crew can become desensitized to the smell of garbage they pick up daily, teachers can become desensitized to dysfunctional classroom behaviors that present themselves throughout the day. These inconsistencies within the education system were beginning to reveal my feelings of anger. The ongoing issues within my own household only added to the situation. I did not pay almost $200 for a teacher exam and have thousands of dollars in student loan debt only to be disrespected and not appreciated for being an educator. That night when I laid my head down to rest I decided that I was sick and tired of being sick and tired. I came to the conclusion that I was going to *quit*.

The next day during Guided Reading, instead of teaching the students phonemic awareness and comprehension skills, I found myself searching for a job that would alleviate the immediate headache I received when I stepped into my class-room. The passion I had for teaching was at an all-time low, and I was completely unmotivated. I reminded myself of my reasons for being in education and how I chose this profession to help educate people about the amazing opportunities around them, but that was not enough to jumpstart my motivation for teaching. My students that day were sensitive to the events that happened throughout the week with Mr. Grumpy and Ms. Sugar and made sure they were on their best behavior. There was one student who always paid attention to my mannerisms. She is an intelligent and bright young lady, and on this particular day she wrote me a letter in a purple marker. It said verbatim, "*I know it has only been a few weeks but I still want to thank you for being a great teacher and cool too! and remember this: The most beautiful things in the world cannot be seen or even touched, they must be felt with the heart.*" A large tear began to swell in the corner of my eye, but I refused to let it fall. That kind gesture from one of the sweetest individuals I have ever met gently reminded me why I started in this profession. I could not allow this present moment of darkness that was caused by a few individuals ruin my overall vision of the greatness the other students in my classroom were attempting to achieve. Within that moment, I knew that if I wanted to create a true change within my classroom and inspire the next generation of world leaders, I would have to change how things were being run in Bonnerville.

4

"Come to the Office"

> "If we always do what we've always done,
> we will get what we've always got."
> —Adam Urbanski

Most teachers will happily admit the number of decisions they make per day could quantitatively translate into the thousands. With that much of a workload, a break is beyond necessary. Summer break for most of us is the time that we rest and rejuvenate ourselves for the upcoming year. Most professionals from other fields are envious of this summer break due to the misconception that we have three months of sun, traveling, and free time to ourselves. That option is for a small percentage of educators who have the luxury of taking a break. *The Huffington Post* reported data from the National Center for Education Statistics that about 16 percent of teachers nationwide are forced to work a second job outside the school system. In North Carolina, however, that number is closer to 25 percent—the third-highest in the entire country. When you include teachers who take second jobs within the school system, more than half of North Carolina educators—*a full 52 percent*—work second jobs to supplement their salaries[1].

As the summer began and Drake's hit record "Summer Sixteen" blasted on the radio, I knew that I could not afford to take a break. In fact, on the contrary, now would be the perfect time to reflect on the different dynamics that were circulating inside of my classroom. I believe in order for one to truly grow and make a change, there must be an awareness of one's own thinking process and the strength to trust an individual to help you identify your weaknesses. Throughout my three years in education, there were many individuals I could have asked to critique my pedagogy and my effectiveness as a high-quality teacher. But there was one individual who was tattooed on my conscience as I attempted to change my classroom and become the true definition of an educator.

Anybody who has worked at a Title I school can attest to the multiple changes that happen within the administration and teacher positions. This was the end of my third year as a beginning teacher and I was on my third administrator. South Greenville was slowly turning around our school culture by adjusting systematic issues that were affecting student growth. But the rate of proficiency at our school really began to increase when Lakeesha Lynch walked through the door. Ms. Lynch is about 5-foot-3 and weighs only 130 pounds, but when she opens her mouth to speak, the room quickly quiets down. Because of the wealth of knowledge she possesses pertaining to the education system, her ability to identify a problem and provide a solution quickly earn respect from educators. She has two graduate degrees, is National Board Certified, and is currently working on her doctorate degree. Despite being an administrator at a low performing school and excelling in her course work, she still manages to keep the school running in tip-top shape. Because her love of education was so evident in how she daily approached her job, I knew immediately she would be the one to sit down with me and hold me accountable for the young minds within my classroom. This confirmation that Ms. Lynch was the right individual with whom I could be transparent did not happen because she rode a magical unicorn from the sky with a $1,000 gift card to the largest online educational resource store (which is Teachers Pay Teachers). I knew that I could be honest about my desires to become a better teacher because her track record proved she was successful in this profession. Her knowledge and sincere desire to create a better school culture created a comfort zone inside which my internal aspirations could thrive.

People often have the wrong perspective on what is important in life. Some say that money is the most important tool we can have in our possession. Hypothetically speaking, if the richest man in the world had a son dying from a terminally ill disease, he would be able to surround the child with the best doctors and care. But once the child passes, money becomes obsolete because he cannot purchase more time for his beloved heir. That analogy leaves us to understand that *time* is the most valuable currency that we have. For anybody to wake up every day to work a job they absolutely hate without any thoughts on what they can do to change is not only embarrassing, it's disgraceful. Specifically, it's embarrassing when you take into account the many individuals who cringe because of the missed opportunities in life where they failed to maximize their time. Because of my keen awareness of maximizing every second of the day, I scheduled a meeting with Ms. Lynch to pick her brain. I openly communicated my thoughts and frustrations about being a teacher and how I desired to return to the classroom the next year with a newfound tenacity. She applauded me for the willingness to have this type of conversation with her and we immediately dove into key aspects of my pedagogy that would help me become better. We analyzed areas that most teachers are not comfortable addressing; for example, in my case, that's lesson plans. During every evaluation, she asked for them and wanted to see data to support the critical decisions within my classroom. Most importantly, Ms. Lynch knew about my charismatic personality and how I could engage any audience, but specifically addressed if there was any instructional substance behind my student engagement.

Often inside the classroom, there are unique battles between student engagement and the rigor a teacher implements into the lessons. If you sway more towards student engagement, you miss the opportunity for students to take something away from your lesson. If you lean more towards differentiated instructional rigor without proper student engagement, you will find yourself sounding like a broken record because you have to constantly repeat the directions to the activity in order for students to comprehend what you are saying. These are the types of situations that most educators face every day, but with everything in life, there must be a healthy balance of the two in order for success to happen. Ms. Lynch and I continued this conversation for almost 15 to 30 minutes and, to be honest, I made sure I wrote down every weakness she identified. I was excited about this journey I was going to embark on and most importantly, the key factor was that *I* wanted this transformation for myself more than my administrator or coworker.

Just because an individual is busy trying to achieve a task does not mean they are being productive at achieving their goal. Being busy does not equate to being successful, and the same could be said about those trying to implement change. Change is constantly happening all around us, but that does not mean that effective change is happening towards the necessary goal. You see, the unique thing about change within any profession is that most people love to talk about what should be done or what could work better, but they lack the mental fortitude and perseverance to bring about that targeted change. People often communicate theories and statistical data on failing schools and what we should do to create change within those environments, but it is rare that you see administrators and teachers stick around for the allotted time to enforce those beliefs. At the beginning of every year you'll see social media doused with fitness goals, the enrollment for gym memberships begins to skyrocket, and most individuals are pumped with adrenaline to accomplish their goals. But most of those people would admit that they become inconsistent with their diet and workout regimen within the first week to a month. I wanted to make sure that I was not one of those educators who fall into the continuous cycle of being pumped up only for the moment about teaching, but later on allow that fire to sizzle out. Mediocre teachers talk about their goals, but highly qualified and effective educators follow through with their action plan on how to achieve their goals.

Planning with the end in mind is a critical component to having success in life. You must first develop a vision of where you are trying to go and be responsible for your actions to reinforce the goals you have set for yourself. I saw myself being a successful teacher before the 2016–2017 school year started after meeting with my administrator. Deep down inside, I knew that I was going to come into the school year with a revitalized mindset and a newfound perspective of how to approach education, specifically at South Greenville Elementary. Whatever you perceive about your school, students, or community will be your reality and furthermore, will affect how you behave. I wanted to make sure I changed my mindset *first* because perception eventually becomes reality.

On August 8, 2016, I posted an Instagram photo of myself and my kids that stated, "This school year will be phenomenal to say the least." And now that I reflect upon that year, I noticed that the meeting with Ms. Lynch and my attitude to want to do better directly correlated to that year. The conference with Ms. Lynch was supplemental to my journey evaluating my thinking process and self-reflection I embarked upon. From our discussion, I took away four critical aspects to being an educator that would not only change my classroom, but also bring about an unforgettable opportunity and change to my community. Each ideology reinforces critical components that educators can continuously work on throughout the year, including oneself. They are not "quick-fix" solutions because they require time and effort in order to see any success. Often, educators are overwhelmed by the need to make numerous decisions and there is a constant search for solutions that will relieve us of the problems we face.

I argue that there is *not* a quick-fix solution in education, but there is an answer to some of the problems we face daily within the classroom. There is an intrinsic detail within our human character that separates failing teachers from successful teachers. That characteristic is called—consistency. When you support effective strategies with consistent effort, success within your classroom (and your personal life) is bound to happen. When I made the personal decision to apply consistency with the four paradigms listed in the next four chapters, that is when true magic began to take place within my own classroom and created a world of endless possibilities for my students.

5

Ron Clark Who?

"One person with passion is better than
forty people merely interested."
—E. M. FORSTER

The ice slowly melted off my windshield as I waited for
my car to warm up. It was a chilly day in January and the
students had just left the school building to go home. I popped
in my auxiliary cord, guided my way to one of my favorite Apple
music playlists, and allowed the tunes to serenade me as I set
my car on cruise control to go home. As I reflected on the school
day, I thought of the different things I could have done to engage
my students in my classroom. We were covering text features in
guided reading, and my students were not grasping the content.
I found myself either repeating the directions multiple times
or noticing that most kids were not engaged in the content at
all. Instead of my classroom feeling like an educational oasis,
from the expression on my students' faces and formative assessments, my classroom was more of a parched desert.

As I arrived at my apartment, I threw on some sweatpants and plopped down on my uncomfortable college-era futon. That was all I could afford since I was still in the process of a legal separation from my wife. As I opened my Instagram application and went to the explore page, a video caught my eye. In this particular video, there was a well-dressed, medium-built Caucasian man surrounded by about eight African-American kids, and they were participating in a popular dance challenge. I probably watched that video about four to five times, jealous that my 6-foot-5 frame could not move in such a fluid manner. Immediately I was intrigued, trying to figure out who this man in the video—who had the audacity to be dancing with students in a classroom—was. That was unheard of in my educational courses.

As I continued to watch the video, I noticed it was not the widescreen smart board that was behind them as they moved in a poetic manner to a popular hip-hop song that drew my attention. Nor was it the beautiful mural that was painted on the classroom wall. It was the *relationship* and *connectivity* between him and the students that spoke so profoundly to me through the art of videography. I immediately began reading the comments, searching for who this man was, and right away, I began learning a lot of information about Ron Clark. I looked at his movie via YouTube and began to understand his journey and how he was able to start the prestigious Ron Clark Academy (RCA) with the elegant educational juggernaut herself, Kim Bearden. As the months went on, I found myself looking up different resources about the school and the types of educational techniques they used to make a lasting impact on their students.

Some time passed before I had the opportunity to meet Ron Clark in person, and I quickly understood why Oprah fell in love with him. The passion he has for teaching can be seen exuding from his face when he begins to talk about his students. Educational equity radiated from his philosophy on teaching when he explained the importance of teaching history from all cultures, not just the majority culture. He explained the importance of making text relevant, not for the sake of compliance, but for his students to use the information they learned in order to breathe new life into their self-confidence. Not only did he verbalize his concepts, but every individual of his team supported his vision and maximized every opportunity to make this a reality within their own classrooms. I knew within the first five minutes I spent with him that this guy talked the talk and walked the walk. As I followed him and other educators from RCA throughout the day, I noticed they all had one common trait in every fiber of their being—a passion to educate. In each educator classroom that I stepped into dedication for teaching immediately grabbed me and kept my attention, to the point that I found myself not paying attention to the clock but holding on to every word spoken. I knew personally that this concept would be the first key to unlocking a world of endless possibilities within my classroom.

One of the biggest misconceptions about infusing passion when you teach is understanding how passion bubbles to the surface. A person does not have to stand on a table dancing and teaching in order to show devotion to teaching. A person does not have to stay at work until 7 p.m. to demonstrate their passion for teaching. I have learned over the course of my career and by watching amazing teachers that passion takes the form of the personality within an individual teacher. I have seen teachers who may have a low speaking voice, but their physical movements and excitement about the content they are teaching inspires every student also to be excited about what is going to happen in class that day. We cannot place passion within a defined box and expect every teacher to display the same type of movements as other energetic educators, because that cuts into the unique build and structure of each individual. But we can demand that teachers across America transform their approaches and perspectives about what they are teaching. We can demand that teachers across America begin to understand how paramount our jobs really are, and how we have a daily responsibility to change a student's life. Inside the classroom, a teacher can be compared to a ringmaster at the circus. We educators have the ability to put on a show that will wow the masses and leave them with memories they can share with their grandkids. Or we have the potential to create a disaster in our classroom where learning isn't happening and students leave the same way they came in 180 days ago.

I have learned from my own classroom experiences as I attempted to restructure the town of Bonnerville that students ultimately *do* care about where you direct your passions. I absolutely *love* teaching second grade math. It could be because there are no complex algebraic equations involved or critical formulas for students to remember. It could be the joy of pulling out fake money and seeing the kids react; that is always entertaining, to say the least. The way you can apply real-life concepts and situations to create better student awareness and understanding is endless when it comes to numbers. But when it came to guided reading, well, that was a completely different story. Guided Reading is *so* similar to shooting free throws. You have to find a consistent and effective routine to enforce in order to see progress. In layman's terms, it took me a while to develop this routine and it often left me frustrated. The amount of time it took to develop four guided reading plans for four different groups seemed like it consumed most of my weekends during the schoolyear. With maintaining numerous running records, creating engaging stations so that students would not get distracted while simultaneously keeping my attention on the guided reading group at my table was a complex task.

My lack of passion for teaching reading began to infiltrate my classroom culture and before I knew it, my students were complaining when it was time to go to their reading stations. And for a moment, in ignorance, I sat frustrated, believing it was *their* fault that their reading scores were below proficiency and it was *their* lack of motivation that literacy was somehow linked to poverty or *their* parents not reading with them at home. When I came to the realization that students care about what the teacher is most passionate about, things began to change for the better within my classroom. The same way misery has the ability to shift the energy within a room and change the dynamic of relationships, so does the electric force of passion possess the same effect. When *I changed my mind* and started infusing my passion for reading into exciting lessons that were grounded in literacy, when I started pulling Guided Reading books that the students would be interested in reading and strategically linking real world connections to different text, my classroom climate began to improve drastically. Before I knew it, my passion for teaching my children with the content at hand permeated so deeply within our classroom that students began to complain when we *ran out of time* during the reading stations.

With that being said, I have learned that as educators we have the amazing ability to display artificial passion. You know: displaying actions that *appear* like we care for what we are teaching but inside, we could care less. There is a difference between passion fueled by meaningless concepts and true passion that is fueled by understanding the life circumstances surrounding you and your students. Artificial passion will cause you to be excited more about the color of your lesson plan book and bulletin board decorum (than teaching). Feeding your classroom and educational philosophy with artificial passion over an extended period is similar to "nourishing" your body with large amounts of fast food and soda pop. The same way your body will begin to feel sluggish and your chances for health-related diseases skyrocket, the same can be said about classrooms. The more we allow counterfeit passion to infiltrate our classrooms, the more we will see our students respond negatively, and the proficiency percentages within our classroom will drastically plummet. Passion is contagious. Besides, our students have a "phony" meter built within their psyche. They can tell when we truly care about our profession or if are we there simply to *survive*.

Passion was not the only concept that impressed me about the Ron Clark Academy. It is fascinating how every member of the staff can infuse the internal passion that flows throughout the school's vision. Ultimately, this action is transferred to their students and the students daily display the dedication to education that emanates throughout the school.

For a while, the "passion" with which I was infusing my pedagogy was undistinguished, at best. It did not have any educational nutritional value and the data I was collecting on my students reflected this. My lack of authentic passion was a contributing factor to the disastrous third year of teaching I experienced. One definition of insanity is repeating the same actions over and over, yet expecting different results. With all things taken into consideration, I knew that my passion for teaching must be built on a more-structured foundation. I needed the type of passion that could not be changed even if I landed the worst class that ever existed in public education.

Earlier in this book I mentioned my desire to help others break free from the different systematic structures that existed in my hometown. The original goal was to become a NBA player, make a few million dollars, and eventually reinvest that revenue back into my community. The need for diversified small businesses is critical and those would jumpstart the community (and those who live there). Unfortunately, though, because my hoop dreams were not fulfilled, I had to find a different path that would allow me to break the "small-town mentality" in the individuals for whom I cared the most. To this day, every time I drive home I meet a high school classmate or family member who could have had the potential to be so much more if they'd only had access to the knowledge that others in more affluent communities have at their fingertips. That understanding has really transformed my passion for teaching and given me a greater purpose. To know I have the power and the ability to expose my students and others to a diversified portfolio of academic and financial knowledge fortifies me to encourage every student who crosses my path.

When I studied the effects of poverty and how they can traumatize an individual, this cemented another layer of passion into my educational philosophy. We have thrown statistics about poverty around so much that some people have become desensitized to the true damage poverty can cause. For example, one day I was conducting a read-aloud during the mini lesson portion of my Guided Reading block. I was carefully making sure I read each verb and adjective in the book with expression in my voice, in order to create excitement for what was going to happen next. As I was reading the book, I noticed one of the boys in my classroom was crying, with tears streaming down his face. We will call him Mr. Football because he is hands down one of the most athletic eight-year-olds I have ever seen in my entire life. Immediately, I stopped reading the book and I started checking to make sure nobody had struck him in the face while I was showing the pictures in the book. But from the looks on his classmates' faces around him, I knew no physical action was involved. Now, Mr. Football is all boy, meaning before we line up to go to lunch from recess, he will slide in the grass to his spot in line and worry about the scrapes and bruises later. So for a couple of seconds, I was completely dumbfounded by why he was crying, as if somebody was literally stabbing him with a knife. I finally asked Mr. Football, "What is wrong, dude?!" He looked at me with tears streaming from his eyes and simply said only two words, "*I'm hungry.*"

It was at that moment I knew that something had to be done. I have heard of hunger pains before, but to see it on the face of a child who cannot control the quality or amount of food in the family's refrigerator is downright depressing. I quickly ran and grabbed a bag of chips and allowed him to eat those at his seat. For the rest of the day I brainstormed different solutions to prevent this problem from ever happening within my classroom again, but I knew that the financial hole that I would dig myself into trying to pay for food would be too much for me to handle alone. He wasn't the only child in my classroom who was trying to navigate through the conundrum of poverty. I concluded that the logical choice would be for me to come into class the next day and teach like a madman. I had to make sure that *every day*, regardless of how I felt emotionally or mentally, I would arrive at my classroom determined to teach my students with every fiber of my being. Most importantly, I knew that if my passion for teaching could instill a love for learning within Mr. Football and his classmates, their likelihood of pursuing higher education would increase. If their education gave them a chance to break the cycle of poverty, then I would have been successful.

For some teachers, passion may be fueled by other injustices you notice within your class or community. The depth and tenacity to how you approach your students may be driven from a specific circumstance or life tragedy. For some teachers, discovering a dysfunctional thought pattern within yourself hinders your ability to be an effective teacher. By paying attention to that insecurity, you allow it to affect your ability to reach children. You may discover defective systems in the community that serves your students. Whatever anyone's situation may be, we must understand that without authentic and genuine passion fueling our classroom environments, true learning will never take place. As educators, when we neglect to develop and maintain a love for teaching, our ability to affect the lives of students and adults around us quickly diminishes. The fuel power that your students will need when they run out of motivation to learn is predicated upon how much authentic passion you have in your fuel tank. Do not depreciate the massive amount of influence you bring into your classroom. Because reviving your passion is mandatory in order for you to turn your classroom, career, and life around.

6

Who Drives
Your Classroom?

"The goal is to turn data into information,
and information into insight."
—Carly Fiorina

One year I worked at a summer camp for the city of Greenville called Camp Escape. Hands down, it was one of the
most rewarding jobs I have ever participated in, mainly because
I had the amazing privilege of working with individuals with
autism and Down Syndrome. The memories and experiences
I gained from working with those children will forever be
embedded within my heart. We would normally go to the pool
two times during the week so the children could have some
aerobic exercise and to help them cool down from the blistering
summer heat. On one particular day as we all were entering the
pool there was a beautiful lifeguard who was in charge of our
specific area. When she walked out of the pool house, it was as

if time stopped. Everything turned into slow motion around her and I caught myself staring as she took her seat to resume her duties. It easily could have been a scene in a *Baywatch* movie as she strutted along the side of the pool. The wind gently blew through her hair and her body was in pristine shape.

Immediately, I started picking up kids to place in the pool in order to draw attention to my post-college athletic frame. Unfortunately, I could not tell if she was paying attention to us because she had on extremely dark sunglasses. I knew that drastic measures must be taken, so luckily one of the kids threw the ball close to her lifeguard stand and almost hit her. *Bingo!* This was my time to capitalize on the moment and make magic happen. I walked over to her stand and as she tossed the ball to me, I said, "Kids are something else, huh?" We both chuckled and began a conversation, sharing some of our most memorable moments with our campers. Things were going well in my mind given how our conversation was proceeding, so I thought it would be smart for us to exchange numbers.

Later that night, around 8 o'clock, I decided to text her and let her know I enjoyed the conversation we had earlier in the day. She responded by saying, "Thank you," and I proceeded to get ready for the next day of camp. The next day I decided to message her and see how her day was going. She never responded, so I figured that she must have had a busy day protecting children at the pool. I allowed two days to pass and I decided to reach out and text her again. But still, there was no response. Now at this point I began to worry because I assumed we would immediately hit it off based on how strong our vibe was at the pool. I decided not to stress over this particular situation and I went on about my day. The next week, I sent her a message about how I hoped she would have a productive week. By the end of the day, there was still no response. This now numbered three times that I had reached out to her, and I knew the best decision was never to contact her again due to the chances of me being viewed as a stalker. Based on this story, we can safely assume from the evidence that she was clearly not interested, right? The read receipts from my iPhone could count as data that showed she clearly was not interested.

Let us examine the counter narrative of this unique circumstance. When I was blessed with the opportunity to appear on *The Ellen DeGeneres Show* the first time, it was one of the best experiences in my entire life. When I arrived back to the Raleigh-Durham International Airport after my trip, my phone vibrated with an intense fluctuation due to more than 150 text messages and other notifications. Guess who was in the midst of the 150 text messages after six months of no communication? You got it, Ms. *"Bae-watch."* Within this parable, I wanted to highlight how data is analyzed and utilized in our everyday lives even though we are often unaware of this process, and most importantly, how we use this information to make life decisions.

Data is all around us. It can be found in subtle ways or through public reports. As our world continually evolves and becomes more technologically advanced, we will find that it is important to use data to make informed decisions about which direction we as a country should proceed. Investors use data and correlations to determine which stock is most lucrative at the moment. Doctors use evidence-based research studies to help find key indicators and interrelationships in specific diseases they are studying. But in education, you would be shocked by the number of teachers and administrators do not depend on data to make critical decisions in their classrooms and schools. To be honest, I fell victim to this educational malpractice myself. Instead of keeping key data points to drive the instruction in my classroom, I allowed emotions and weak assessments to help me decide what should be taught. Not only was this dangerous for my professional development, but ultimately this pernicious dysfunction was harming the children within my classroom. When I lacked adequate data to support *why* I was teaching specific standards in my classroom or *how* certain students were grouped, this gave students more leeway to behave in a way that was not acceptable because my lessons were not rigorous nor relevant to those assigned groups.

Utilizing data that is relevant in our classrooms gives us the opportunity to better serve our students to help them reach their full academic potential. Now more than ever, we as 21st-century educators should use evidence-based research strategies to better serve our students. We live in a profession where individuals focus more on the "cool" factor behind developing a theory than on implementing methods that have been tested and proven inside the classroom. Personally, I make sure I understand the magnitude of this concept within my own classroom. The students I teach are not only my students, they are somebody's daughters and sons. We must recognize the delicate packages who enter our classroom, handle them with care, and utilize strategies that have been proven to be effective for the diverse demographics that we serve.

In my third year of teaching, I remember administering formative and summative assessments that were given to my students only for the sake of compliance with the district and the state. If we are brutally honest, a lot of school districts have designed schedules that overload students with multiple assessments. This not only creates student burnout, but simultaneously for some educators, the feedback from these assessments just sits on our desks without proper evaluation. I did not understand the power of data until I began to analyze the information provided by my students. I am not talking about just looking at the students who were proficient, but properly digging through the item analysis to make informed decisions upon the directions to take my classroom.

Properly looking at each data point within an assessment gives teachers the chance to discover positive or negative correlations on how students may be performing. By examining the test data, teachers should be able to look at the various strengths and weaknesses of students in their classroom. This is vital for two important reasons. The first reason is that proper analysis of the scores will help us form small groups of students, which are critical for empowering our instruction. There will always be different styles of learners within our classrooms who are on different levels within any given subject area. Effectively using the scores from any formative or summative assessment will allow you to group students who could benefit from your pedagogy in order to better assist their learning. For the first three years of my educational career, I struggled in Guided Reading due to my inability to properly use data to build successful Guided Reading groups. At its face value, I could see what level a student was on and would group accordingly. I constructed a group off their overall proficiency scores, but individuals within a group had different struggles. In my higher group, even though all five of my students were reading on a specific level, three of them struggled more with phonemic awareness and the other two struggled with the ability to understand the written comprehension part of the test. I did not begin to see success within my classroom until I started digging down into their provided scores and analyzing the specific reading skills the individual lacked.

The second reason we should examine test data more closely is because different assessments will help us figure out which students need additional services in our classroom. I often pray for the exceptional children (EC) department in my school because the number of referrals they receive each year, without proper data explaining why the child is being referred, is quite daunting. Within my classroom, I had a student who appeared academically low based upon an eye test. As the school year went along, I looked at his scores to confirm that he was performing below grade level, but I never took it a step further than simply placing him into small groups so I could have the chance to work with him more closely. As the school year progressed, I recognized that it was *my* educational responsibility not to allow this individual to fall through the cracks within my classroom. I had to make a personal decision that collecting the right data on this student and implementing evidence-based interventions would be the only way to determine this student's proper diagnosis. Without proper analyzation of the data, it is nearly impossible to identify what's happening with a student. Some students perform poorly due to lack of motivation within the classroom. The student may be battling a learning disability or the child may need to be put through the MTSS (Multi-Tiered System of Supports) process to determine if that student should be admitted into the special education department. By properly understanding the importance of using data and breaking down specific correlations within the numbers, we can place ourselves in a better position as educators not only to serve students, but also help identify the obstacles that may be hindering their learning experience.

All this sounds good, right? I am sure you have heard it in your professional development before, but I understand your train of thought as you read this chapter. I am a teacher also and I fully understand the workload we encounter every single day. It is emotionally and mentally exhausting. It seems as if individuals from the state level, district level, and administration continue to pile many educational duties for us to fulfill without taking anything off our plate. And now I am come along, asking you to take more time out of your day to sit down and look at count-less reports and stacks of papers that need to be graded? Well, to bring you comfort, I am from the school of thought that we as teachers must find a way to work *smarter* and not *harder*. We are constantly charged with the task of making the impossible possible within our classroom. This type of job can easily place us in the position of having a mental breakdown if we do not find ways of performing our daily duties without burning out. I have discovered three programs that allow me to collect data safely, communicate with parents more effectively, and, most important, provide the proper documentation I need to utilize data in a more efficient way within my classroom. The unique factor about each program is that each does not require paper or pencil, but all the programs or applications can be accessed consistently through technology.

Behavior management within a school system is always a priority based off the premise that in order for a teacher to be able to pour his or her passion and pedagogy into the classroom, there must be order among the students. When it comes to providing data on a student's behavior within the classroom, it is difficult to provide a hard copy of anecdotal notes written over a period of time when, for the most part, you are writing names down on a whiteboard for student consequences. Or, if you are into printing a behavioral checklist, you may run into the problem of keeping up with the amount of paperwork on that specific student as time goes by. Class Dojo is a program that can be run from any smartphone or device that has a web browser or access to the app store. An advantage for this program being accessible on a device is that it keeps important confidential documentation in one place. I have found that the use of Class Dojo in my classroom has been monumental for three main reasons.

First, parents can track their students' behavior in real time throughout the day. This allows immediate feedback without a teacher being pulled from their instructional time to call a parent. Parents who are heavily involved in their child's schoolwork often appreciate this convenience because students love to switch up stories about what happened at school. Second, Class Dojo allows you to diversify and categorize the types of behaviors that are acceptable within your classroom. Each behavior can either be positively or negatively rewarded based on the amount of points you are willing to give the student. This creates a healthy competition among students within the class-room to see who can earn the most points by their good behavior throughout the day. Third, Class Dojo has a data system that is second to none when tracking student behaviors throughout the year and providing meaningful detailed reports. Each day, the program calculates the student behaviors into a percentage and stores this number. You can pull reports from the previous day, previous month, or even the previous year. This type of information is critical during parent conferences to show the progression or regression of their child and specific behaviors that must be addressed. Also, the detailed reports may help a struggling student by identifying specific interventions that can help improve a child's school behavior in order for them to succeed within the classroom.

The second application that I use for proper documentation and to keep in constant contact with parents is called Remind. Remind is a messaging app that helps teachers, students, and parents communicate quickly and through a smooth interface. Remind is a company that is fully invested in teachers, educa-tional equity, and creating an infrastructure that is efficient for the individuals who utilize this program. I had the opportunity to chat with Remind leaders at their headquarters and with cofounder David Kopf about the foundational motivation for starting his company. David explained that he started Remind because, as a student with ADD and dyslexia, his brother Brett *struggled* to stay organized. In an automated world, he wondered, why can't I just receive reminders before assignments and exams? So they built a prototype, then partnered with the telecommunications department at Michigan State University to run a survey.

What they found was both encouraging and misleading. Over half the students reported that without Remind, they would have forgotten an exam or assignment; nearly all said they would continue using it. The misleading part came when the Kopf brothers actually built the program. Some students never quite got around to signing up.

The brothers struggled for three years to get the app operational and accepted. What they learned from those three years of struggle is that the best way to help students is by helping teachers. Teachers provide leveraged impact, not only in the context of Remind but to the education system as a whole. In the United States, there are 100 million students and parents. If Remind truly was to help educators, they must first sign them all up. It would be easier to build something that 3.7 million teachers really love that solves their problems than to sign up 100 million students and parents.

Today, Remind is one of the most widely used apps in the United States education system, with active teachers in more than 70 percent of U.S. schools and 23 million active monthly users. This simple premise, to help students by helping teachers, extends beyond the application to the education system as a whole. "Teachers are a rising tide that lifts all boats," David says. "We've captured this in one of our three values, which is 'Teacher Obsessed,' and reinforced it with our vision, 'to give every student the opportunity to succeed,' which aligns with that of our teachers. To be clear, what we do *not* believe is that technology will improve education; rather, we believe technology can help *people* improve education. And that is Remind, an app that helps *people* improve education. It does so very simply, by fostering connections—it helps people build relationships."

I have continued important conversations about education, data, and building relationships since our initial meeting. The Kopf brothers's and their amazing team's dedication to teachers has relieved the stress of maintaining communication with parents as documentation. It is comforting to know that David and Brett are not biased towards an individual's ethnicity or gender, but, are focused on creating a better world by providing pristine service to educators and other professional sectors.

Remind prides itself on three core values that allow the company to wholeheartedly serve educators. First, they are teacher-obsessed and systematically make it a priority to partner with teachers to earn their trust. Second, they understand the unique power that their program brings to the education field and they focus on making an impact by always finding a solution. Third, they create simplicity for others by making sure their program is advanced enough to handle the workload of many different professions, but also by providing simplicity through their user interface. A beautiful concept about Remind is that it provides a security measure that prevents parents or others from discovering your personal phone number. You cannot make phone calls through this application, but you can send messages quickly and notify every parent or student within your classroom collectively or individually. This program has worked for me in many different circumstances and situations, especially when I need to provide evidence for parent contact in an evaluation or send a mass text to parents about homework assignments that may be due throughout the week.

The last program that I utilized (and even convinced one of my school administrators to invest in) is called Mastery Connect. Other than dealing with some individuals who may be unstable parents, the long, monotonous weeks of testing, or the tough behaviors that seem to multiply towards the end of the year, what is the biggest pain-in-the-butt you deal with as a teacher? Grading papers. All across America (and even the world) there is a teacher who has a large stack of papers that need to be graded in order for the data to be utilized. For a while, I had this problem and struggled to find a way to grade papers on a timely schedule and provide adequate feedback to students and parents. For a season, our weekly PLC meetings (Professional Learning Communities, where we discuss student data and the next steps to improve learning) were incorrectly used for grading papers instead of comparing our data points. Mastery Connect not only solves the problem of grading papers, but the program assists teachers by connecting them to other educators around the world to empower collaboration. Mastery Connect has found a distinctive way of making learning simple for students by providing teachers with different levels of understanding, targeting students for intervention, and tips on improving learning and instruction. They offer four main pillars that create a strong foundation for their program and lift some of the weight off a teacher's shoulders.

First, the mastery tracker gives teachers the ability to assess and track state and Common Core standards in real time. Second, the resource pins allow you to have access to different curriculum maps for improved instruction. Next, due to the large community that exists within this program, Mastery Connect gives you access to 30,000 different standard aligned assessments that other educators use that have been starred by how effective and popular they are. The last advantage of this program is my favorite! They have developed a grading tool that provides instant grades by utilizing the camera on your smartphone, tablet, or computer webcam. The program generates a bubble sheet and a unique identification number for each student, and by scanning the bubble sheet with your device, the program automatically grades the assessment and alerts you of the status of your student. Grading papers use to take me at least 30 minutes to an hour, but now, I can move through a stack of papers within three to five minutes, tops.

The programs I mentioned are not a "one-size-fits-all" solution for the educational system. I understand the complexity of switching systems in your classroom and trying to identify different ways to differentiate it for your teaching style and students. Trust me, *I get it*. But I also know how it feels to be lost within your own classroom trying to figure out a way to help students grow and provide academic rigor. You cannot state that you want to increase the learning rate within your classroom if you are unwilling to dive into data to find a more effective way of collecting data from your students. If you want to really see your classroom transform, we have to agree upon this premise. If we make the breakdown of efficient and valid data in our classrooms a priority, from there we can begin seeing class-rooms that breed emotional and academic success. Because by collecting meaningful and informative data, potent small groups and dynamic lessons can be brought forth.

7

Relationships
Before Content

"If kids come to us from strong,
healthy-functioning families, it makes our job easier.
If they do not come to us from strong,
healthy-functioning families,
it makes our job more important."
—Barbara Colorose

In my third year of teaching, there was a really handsome
young man in my classroom whom all the little girls and
teachers used to swoon over. From their reactions, he was a
sight for sore eyes, but sometimes in my classroom the only
thing he made my eyes do was roll into the back of my head
because he wouldn't pay attention to my lessons. We are going to
name him Mr. Ladies Man for the sake of this conversation. He
was a peculiar individual and was always interested in crafting
different mechanisms out of paper. I firmly believe he will go on

in life to become either an engineer or computer software creator because of his ability to generate amazing ideas on the go. Now Mr. Ladies Man was a sweet kid with an even temperament. He possesses this gentle smile that always invites anybody to come and have a conversation with him. I enjoyed having him in my classroom because he was one of those students who create a healthy balance for the classroom climate.

On this particular day, something was off in regards to his demeanor. He did not speak when he entered the classroom like he normally did, and he went to his seat and placed his head down. I assumed he had a rough night due to how large his family was and he probably did not receive an adequate amount of sleep, so I allowed him to sleep during our morning work. This unconventional strategy proved to be effective after he awoke because he was ready to rock and roll for reading. What I did not know is that this behavior would continue or the next couple of days and the amount of time he would sleep began to increase. The volcano of frustration was beginning to simmer inside of me because I had been in PLC and grade level meetings for hours planning this lesson to make sure he would become a better reader, but all he wanted to do was come into my classroom and sleep. The audacity of this kid! The next morning when I arrived for work, I was determined to let him know about himself and correct this behavior. Sure enough, he walked into my classroom and placed his head down and within five minutes, he fell right to sleep. I quickly walked over and tapped his shoulder and began to bear down upon him, questioning his inability to stay awake in my classroom. His answer shook me to my core.

See, Mr. Ladies Man has six other siblings who live with his single mother. If you ask him, he has no idea where his father is located. During this time, somehow, they were kicked out of their apartment and were staying in a one-bedroom hotel room approximately five minutes from the school. The reason why he was so sleepy is because he was sharing a bed with two or three other siblings. He was not trying to listen to my lesson about utilizing place value blocks to assist in solving math problems or the importance of using text features to comprehend a passage. His main focus was to get a chance to close his eyes and rest. I went into the hallway and for the first time in my career as a teacher, I felt a tear coming from my eyes. I am not an emotional individual, but this situation was beyond my ability to comprehend. I was perplexed by the number of obstacles he had to overcome, not only to make it to school, but the fight to keep his attention span alive in order to receive any information. To be frank, if I would have engaged in meaningful conversations with him more consistently, the problem Mr. Ladies Man was engrossed in could have been resolved more quickly.

It was at this moment that I understood that being a teacher is more than bragging to your colleagues about how many kids are proficient on the state exam or building cute little notebooks that students can utilize that add work to their portfolio. Those things have their place, but this particular moment showed me that teaching is far more complex than the standards that are handed to us to instill within children. In fact, it can be argued that school is more about the lasting relationships you build with the students in your classroom that determine their success in the school year and later in life.

One of the greatest life lessons I have learned as an adult and teacher is that it is important for us to get out of our own experience. What I mean by this statement is that it is extremely important that we understand that every student we meet does not have the same upbringing as any one of us. For some, their environment at home may be ideal. The child has both parents present in the home, they live in a safe neighborhood, and they have the available resources to supplement the education they are receiving from one of the top schools in the county. For other students, they may have the exact opposite. One—or no—parent may be present, they live in government housing, and if they do not attend the summer feeding programs, they may go hungry. I have taught students who were in the foster care system and witnessed how that situation gravely affected how open they were to trusting new people who came into their life. In my class-room, I have experienced the whiplash from young men without fathers who despise the very presence of an authoritative male figure. They crave having a father-to-child relationship, but they do not have the proper tools to communicate those feelings. I also have had the opportunity to teach students from the more affluent side of life. You know, the students who take better vacations for Christmas and spring break than you do (and *you* are the teacher?). In all those experiences, I have learned that whichever side of the tracks your students come from, it is essential to understand that before we start pushing for true magic to happen within our classroom, there must be a healthy connection established between the student and the teacher.

I want you to imagine that students are similar to the plastic food storage containers that you use to pack your favorite

Thanksgiving meal before you leave your family on the holidays. Now before you can put your most favorite and tantalizing meals inside of the container, you must first remove the lid in order for the process to begin. It would be a tragedy and quite embarrassing for you to place your mother's famous, mouthwatering, baked macaroni and cheese on top of the container without opening the lid first. That same concept that works packing your favorite dish in order to reap the benefits of it later can be applied to how we as educators must first remove the lid of unfortunate circumstances in order to deposit knowledge that can be used and savored at a later time in order to satisfy educational hunger pains.

Due to the complexity of personalities that students bring into the classroom, it is essential to understand that most students come with different layers of dysfunction that have been developed and repeated before they arrive at your door. It is necessary for educators to understand that there is a timed process that we must endure in order to establish a positive student-teacher relationship with our pupils. I like to ascribe this situation to the analogy of an individual digging for oil. Do you remember the cartoons back in the day where the workers were drilling for oil in the ground and as soon as the oil springs up there was a huge celebration because they were now wealthy? I think this is the best analogy to describe the perfect picture of teachers trying to build substantial relationships with their students. But there is something critical in the analogy about drilling for oil that I want to highlight. In relationship building, there is a long, tedious process of individuals utilizing strategies and loud machinery to dig through tough material in order to reach the wealth of knowledge that is buried beneath the surface. Often, students in our classrooms present a hard, external layer of mistrust and life tribulations, but before we can properly impart instructional content, we must take the time to dig through the hardened layers of circumstantial situations to break through to the richness of student proficiency.

During this drilling process, I have learned that digging for the wealth of potential beneath the surface is where most teachers burn-out before building effective relationships with their students. Educators burn-out digging through multilayers of life circumstances that students bring. It is not easy and is often a job that many do not endure to the end. The long hours of finding ways to break through to a student often leave the teacher exhausted and further discourages the educator from building an important relationship. If we as teachers could understand that, even though this process is tedious and strenuous, the end goal is far greater than the present troubles we face trying to build successful relationships with our students.

This context can be applied to the conversation of how there is sometimes a struggle between Caucasian teachers and African-American students, or vice versa. I recently had the opportunity to speak with some educators at a beginning teacher engagement; after some pictures, this sweet Caucasian lady approached me. She pulled me to the side and began by saying, "I would love for you to be as transparent and honest with me. I would really appreciate if you could tell me why my African-American students are so mean to me, especially my girls. I have worked hard to build relationships with them and earn their trust, but it seems as if it is not working." I paused for a moment so I could analyze the situation without any background knowledge of the students. As I worked through my thoughts and personal experiences, I had seen this problem before within my own school system, which is predominately black. So my response to her was simplistic, but key. Just like the drilling for oil analogy I referenced above, I explained to her that digging to cultivate a relationship with them will take longer than 180 days.

Some students have years of mistrust towards teachers, the majority culture, and memories of different individuals locked away in their subconscious. We live in a world that revolves around social media and the timeframe it takes us to access information is faster than ever. Students are aware of the racial tensions that are no longer subtle in our everyday lives. The fact that we had a presidential election were some people were emboldened to share their hate and disgust for other cultures did not make matters better for students and teachers within the education system.

I also informed her she must take into account that there were teachers before her. Unfortunately, we do not know if they attempted to show the amount of love towards her students she has been trying to display or whether the previous teacher showed bias within his/her teaching methods. I ended my advice to her by simply saying, "Keep drilling." Because eventually, she will have a breakthrough with her students and it will be rewarding to see how far her students will go for her.

There is no doubt that times have changed in regards to the display of disrespect within the school systems. It is not uncommon to see students blatantly disrespecting teachers and creating larger relational barriers for educators to break through before they can begin teaching the assigned content. My mother, who is a guidance counselor, shared some advice with me recently something that resonated deeply within me and has become embedded in my educational philosophy. She said, "At one point in time, a teacher's sole purpose was to simply educate his or her students. But now, if an individual wants to become an educator in the 21st century, they must also be cognizant of the fact that they will also have the duty of being a parent, psychologist, and doctor, and uphold the personal responsibility of being a positive role model." Carrying multiple job titles—and responsibilities—while only receiving compensation for one can be quite frustrating. But we as educators must understand that our focus should remain on the overall success of our children rather than the daily battles that we fight within our classrooms. If we can find a way to be patient while building relationships with our students, the end reward is worth it.

There was an adorable student I used to have in my class who could turn anybody's frown into a smile. She was smaller than most of her classmates, which added points to her adorable factor, and she loved dancing. Whenever you turned on music, her eyes would light up with joy and you could see genuine happiness radiate from her face because she was able to participate in something she loves to do. She was very skilled in mathematics and understanding the science of comprehension behind mathematical word problems. One day she came into the classroom and her whole countenance was completely opposite of what I normally saw. As we began the math lesson, I noticed she was not as engaged and was standoffish when answering questions. When it came time to work in collaborative pairs with her best friend I noticed that she refused to work, she had crossed her arms in a guarded position, and she had a melancholy look on her face. I have learned as an educator that when a child shows strong external emotions that shifts the climate inside the classroom, something serious has happened and must be carefully investigated. I brought her over to my desk to chat, and instantly her small frame gently fell into my arms and she began sobbing. For about five minutes, I just simply hugged her. While her classmates were at their seats focusing on their independent work, she revealed to me that her parents were involved in an enormous fight and, unfortunately, she had the misfortune of listening to the entire argument before school. While fighting back more tears, she explained she'd heard her mother say she'd never step foot inside the house again. To be seven years old, I am sure the thought of her parents deciding not to be together anymore was painful to even think about. The pain in her eyes is something that I will never forget.

For the rest of the day I simply kept an eye on her and made sure that I overloaded her with positive affirmations. I knew that this was a critical moment in her life; if I did not capitalize on this moment to deepen our relationship, she would most likely fall behind in her class work. With my mother's advice floating around in my mind, I decided that I would give her a hug in the morning, at recess, and at the end of the school day. This is a simple strategy on the surface, but the social, emotional benefits would be worth the investment. There was a specific reason why I was doing this, but to her, it was her teacher simply caring for her in a time of need. I continued this practice for almost three weeks to show consistency and to reinforce that she knew I truly cared about her well-being. Eventually, she returned to her normal state because I made the conscious decision to intentionally and genuinely care for her first and to teach her the necessary standards second.

Developing relationships before content is probably the most difficult thing in regards to perfecting our approach to the art of teaching. Human-to-human interactions have never been easy due to the many types of circumstances, differences, and other relationships we build with other individuals. As educators, we teach students specific procedures and strategies to deal with the dysfunction that they face outside our classrooms, but we often ignore that students have to return to that same toxic environment at the end of the day. With this understanding, there will always be a natural tug-of-war over a child's mind as they transition between two totally opposite environments each day. This confirms that when we use strategies within a classroom, whether they involve the academic or behavioral arena, patience must be exercised in order for us to see a true transformation. The student-teacher relationship requires a delicate approach. Any false motive or any action that can be misinterpreted could be detrimental and possibly cause more disruption within our classrooms. Mr. Grumpy and Ms. Sugar are two examples of past students who to this day continually reach out to me and will adhere to any advice or request that I make. I firmly believe that the relationship that I have cultivated with these two students would not be as fruitful if I had never exercised patience in order to strengthen our relationship. If we as educators continue to cultivate relationships before stuffing standards and assessments into our children's school experience, we will then see a shift in our classroom culture that leads to student success.

8

Take Your Shot

"Obstacles don't have to stop you.
If you run into a wall, don't turn around and give up.
Figure out how to climb it, go through it,
or work around it."
—MICHAEL JORDAN

I want to share a story as an example for how often educators
have the potential to create an amazing world of opportunities
in their classrooms, but because of fear, they limit themselves. It
could be fear from what your coworkers may say or insecurity
that your idea may not be well received by other individuals.

Let's return to my college basketball career at Winston-
Salem State University. Although I did not receive lots of playing
time in my freshman year, adjusting to collegiate basketball at
the Division I level was more difficult than I anticipated. This
varied from the amount of talent on the other teams (Iman
Shumpert, Kent Bazemore, Jeff Teauge, Al-Farouq Aminu,
and so on) to balancing my extracurricular activities with my

academic studies. It was not easy for me to manage the amount of pressure to perform, and it seemed only to add up to a greater weight upon my young shoulders. But I knew this was something I must conquer despite the new amount of responsibility I was experiencing. December 20, 2008, is a day that changed the direction of my basketball career. We were facing the Avrett Rams and I knew this would be my perfect opportunity to break out of the shooting slump I was in. My mother and my youngest sister, Khailah, drove four hours to support me, so it was only right that I try to go out and perform to the best of my ability. We were about to get out for Christmas break and this was our very first home game. Students and many different individuals from the community packed the Gaines Center at Winston-Salem State University to show support.

As the game started, I sat on the side of the bench waiting for the coach to call my number. As the game progressed towards the end of first half, the coach turned to me and said, "Let's go, Mike!" I jetted off the bench into the game like a horse beginning the Kentucky Derby. My mindset going into the game was to be super aggressive, to attack the basket. The point guard ran one of our offensive plays, I quickly drove to the basket for a layup, and was fouled on the play. I was feeling good and walked to the free throw line with confidence. I have taken at least 10,000 free throws in my lifetime, whether it was in practice or during a game. This was my chance to finally gain some confidence by seeing the ball go through the basket. As I stepped to the free throw line, I noticed a beautiful young lady in the stands. As a young man in college, she was all the motivation that I needed to try and be the next Lebron James that night. The referee tossed me the ball, and I proceeded to go through my usual free throw routine. Everything felt good until I released the ball. As the basketball left my fingers, it ended up going wide left and completely missed the rim.

For the first time in my life, I shot an air ball and my heart sunk down to my shoes. The crowd busted out in laughter and the opposing team quickly began the air ball chants. I tried to shake off this embarrassing feat, but fear was beginning to creep within my psyche. The referee passed me the ball once again and this time, my free throw shot made a connection between the backboard and the rim. With two badly missed shots on my conscious, I tried to regain my composure, but unfortunately it was too late. My teammates tried to pass me the ball later in the game, but the fear of missing my next shot had me psychologically paralyzed. We ended up winning that basketball game, but for me, I had just taken a catastrophic loss.

Later that week, Coach Garvin sent a text message to me saying he wanted to meet up with me and my teammates for a shooting workout at 5:30 a.m. I reluctantly agreed. As we were going through the workout and I started to warm up, Coach Garvin could still see apprehension in my shot. He approached me with a frown on his face and said, "Michael, are you still scared to shoot the ball?" I lied, and told him my muscles were cold. But he immediately saw through my deception and made this monumental statement, "How can you ever make a shot that you never take? You miss 100 percent of the shots you do not take." As I continued through the workout, I began to understand in a deeper light that he was correct. I allowed one moment to overpower the other successful attempts I had accomplished and imprison me. That is the power of fear—placing you in invisible handcuffs until you decide to become free.

I share this story because the simple fact remains that fear hinders authentic passion and crushes productive relationships. As I think back to that story from college, my mind tends to drift and think about what could have happened if I did not allow myself to fall into the trap of fear. There comes a point when you are sick and tired of being sick and tired. Those were my feelings towards the constant battles I encountered with fear. I finally made the decision that I would not allow the idea of failure to scare me again. Instead, I would try my best to be successful and push towards innovation every chance I could.

When I started the beginning of this school year, I made sure that I integrated the four concepts (passion, data, relationships, and innovation) heavily into my classroom culture. Of course, with every school year there are different challenges and dynamics that educators must adhere to, but these four pillars remained consistent in my classroom. I started the beginning of the school year teaching standard RL.2.1, which covers answering questions pertaining to key details in a text (who, what, when, where, why, and how). This standard also helps second graders strengthen their comprehension skills as they transition into a new school year. My team built a solid lesson plan and I also considered the different levels of readers I had within my classroom. At that point, there were only five out of twenty kids on the second-grade reading level. So much for the idea that everybody comes to school on grade level, right? The task of teaching so many different levels seemed daunting, but I knew if I could differentiate the lesson and pull small groups to the side, the potential for proficiency would increase. We focused on this lesson for approximately two weeks, until I decided to give a summative assessment to calculate who had grown and who was still struggling.

As I began grading the test, I was distraught to note that most of the students in my classroom were failing this assessment. Only two students were proficient on this exam and my brain immediately went into emergency mode. Ms. Lynch once explained to me that if 80 percent of your students fail a summative exam, the problem is not the students, but *you*. I knew that I only had two options in regards to this problem. Number one, I could move on to the next standard and try to fill in the gaps as the year went along. But the problem with that logic is that the Common Core standards work vertically and they would need this foundational skill in order to understand more complex text as we progressed through the year. Or option number two, I could spend a little more time on this standard and find a way to reteach it. Not only just reteach the standard, but find a different method or strategy in order for my students to be successful. Too often, we as teachers spend time reteaching a standard *but we do not adjust the strategies* we used in the previous lesson. Once again, we know that doing the same thing over and over, expecting different results, equals—insanity.

During independent work, I noticed that my students seemed more attentive and enjoyed listening to instrumental music on YouTube. I made sure I played different genres to enhance their musical vocabulary. I used this tactic to help loosen up the classroom environment and to allow them to use music as a tool to relieve hidden stress. On one particular day, a popular hip-hop song called "Cut It" came on and their reaction was priceless. They giggled, laughed, and danced their way through the entire worksheet. I chuckled as I graded their work because shockingly, they all did quite well. So later that night as I was on my futon reflecting on their last summative assessment, I decided to write some lyrics to the hip-hop song that would incorporate the instructional content from the reading standard we were covering. This was my first time this school year attempting this method, but I had learned you do not make 100 percent of the shots you do not take. Now, was it a crazy idea? Yes. Some classrooms look like *Jumanji* was filmed there when some teachers try to play music without the proper procedures. But why not shoot for something different? Why not push the norms and refuse to allow the opinions of others to marginalize the creative power within my classroom? With that understanding lodged in my mind, I was able to rest that night knowing tomorrow would be a chance to actually have fun within my classroom.

The next day I returned to the classroom and I showed the students the lyrics to the song that we would be using. They were ecstatic, overjoyed about something fresh being incorporated within the classroom! The so-called "rappers" and "dancers" in my classroom were elated that I decided to infuse music into a reading lesson. But I did not want to leave out other students in my classroom who were gifted in other areas. They enjoyed the song so much that they started to change the lyrics I originally had, and together they replaced some words with key vocabulary from the standard. This was not the original plan, but what teacher is ignorant enough to stop higher order thinking in their classroom? So I decided to make a deal with them that would incorporate all students and push them to earn this reward. Honestly, I set my expectations high because children need to be pushed by instructional rigor to maximize their learning experience. I called them to attention and said, "If thirteen of you pass this reading assessment on this go-around, I will personally shoot you in a music video to the song that we created for this standard." From their reaction, you would have thought that I had just given each student one thousand dollars, with a year's supply of Sour Patch Kids.

For the next week and a half, my students worked tirelessly and expeditiously moved into reading stations during our classroom lessons. They came together as a family and decided they wanted to achieve this goal to push themselves to a different level of work ethic. This small activity created wonders for my classroom as the assignment guided the students to work together. The reward of a music video taught them the value in positively uplifting their classmates in order to achieve a common goal. The next week, I administered the test the second time and they all waited for me to post the data to see if they had won their prize. When the final results were posted in the classroom, the kids erupted with screams and cheers! Thirteen out of twenty-one students ended up passing the reading assessment the second time around! It was amazing to see them celebrate their victory, but as an educator, it felt good to finally give myself a pat on the back after battling through this standard. Now it was time for me to fulfill my end of the bargain with this music video. I did not have a professional camera, so I simply decided to use my smartphone. I allowed students who were not the best dancers or rappers to sit down and plan the different scenes and footage we would need in order to create the video. In the back of my mind, I was still shocked that they internally motivated themselves to achieve their goal. By that Thursday, we finished the music video and I posted it on Facebook to show my family and friends how my kids exceeded my expectations—and the rest is history.

Some people do not understand the philosophical power of an idea. When it comes to innovation, it is deeper than an individual trying to create something new. Innovation involves an individual who is willing to challenge the societal norms around the particular constructs they interact with daily. One simple idea that came from me trying to find a new way for my students to learn a standard that I taught poorly ultimately created a breath of fresh air for not only my entire school, but for the community of educators throughout the world. Being willing to attempt something new allowed my students, most from poverty-stricken areas, to be introduced to a world of adequate resources, to a new system where they understood that hard work does pay off. If we really begin to dissect the entire situation from the foundation of a music video, we can with authority say that if it weren't for my kids pushing to challenge themselves, the school would not have access to an additional $130,000. The school also would not have 55-inch flat screen TVs, drones, or additional iPads to supplement the classroom instruction. If it weren't for their effort to challenge their own inabilities and insecurities, the positive exposure that South Greenville Elementary received this school year would have never happened.

Due to her amazing spirit and generosity, Ellen DeGeneres decided to fly my entire class to Los Angeles for a second appearance in February. Talk about a field trip of a lifetime! We only had one week from the time the show's producers called to the day we departed Raleigh-Durham International Airport—one week to prepare all the emergency contact paperwork, medicines, and legal forms. This gave us an earthshaking headache for sure, but I kept the excitement of the first-time flyers in my mind. In the end, the entire trip was worth the experience for me, and, more importantly, for my students. I was able to take twenty kids, the majority from low socioeconomic backgrounds, to Los Angeles for an all-expenses paid trip for an entire week. While we were there, the magnitude of the field trip began to hit me and my students in different ways. For a lot of them they were excited about seeing skyscrapers for the first time or experiencing how it feels to take off on an airplane. I still chuckle now at how some of them placed their face in their hands because they were scared.

But for me, the joy of the field trip came from having the opportunity to allow my students to live life as if they were from an upperclass, affluent family. They did not have to worry about what they were going to eat, where they were going to sleep, or even what clothes they were going to wear. For once in their lives, every single last detail was taken care of and they were able to be kids and enjoy the moment. To laugh without a care, to eat until they were full, and to swim until their limbs were numb. Life-changing moments like recording their song at the same studio as Michael Jackson, shooting a music video with Big Sean, and having the opportunity to meet Ellen DeGeneres in person will be memories they will never forget. All because of one idea to find an innovative way to make sure they understood the standard I was teaching.

As I have traveled to different schools and have personally seen amazing lessons from incredible teachers all over the world, I think it is more important than ever for teachers to push our creative muscles to the max. There have been in-depth studies on the many types of learning styles that exist in human nature. With that data, we have the knowledge to push ourselves to generate fresh, rigorous, and engaging lessons to help captivate the brilliant minds of the students who are in our classrooms. Will every great idea or amazing lesson be recognized? Unfortunately, no. But I believe when we as educators focus on innovating concepts within our classroom for the sake of our students and not for the approval/acceptance of others, we will experience true gratification.

For some of us, like myself, creating off-the-wall lessons and projects to intertwine within our lessons is a struggle. The theory of the idea sounds great, but the execution part is where great ideas often die. That is why I stare in amazement at Ron Clark and Kim Bearden or Melissa Fields and Tracy Faircloth, because they have the unique talent to create the most dynamic lessons out of thin air. Luckily in the age of technology, there are endless resources for educators to help assist us in creating a classroom through innovative lessons that bring forth success in our classroom culture. There is nothing wrong with utilizing activities and lessons from Pinterest, blogs, or the most popular resources of all, Teachers Pay Teachers. In fact, every high-quality educator I know encourages this practice. Education is the profession where collaboration makes the individual stronger and better. One famous book states, "Iron sharpens iron," and I stand by that ideology.

We were created as human beings to be interdependent, meaning we will always need somebody to help us move forward in life. Somebody to help us see the blind spots in our path that we so easily ignore. Somebody to assist us in areas where we are weak, not just compliment us on tasks that we do well. If a teacher tries to attempt to be a phenomenal educator by their own strength, they will struggle tremendously as we face the turbulent winds in education. It's similar to an individual trying to grasp a frog with bare hands doused in oil. I am not saying it is not possible, but the percentage of success is extremely low. It is easy for anybody to be a mediocre teacher, but it takes effort, consistency, and long hours to be a teacher who chooses to be innovative in the classroom. I encourage you, as I do with myself, to challenge yourself and realize you are not left to figure out this conundrum called "teaching" alone. Be sure to utilize the resources that are available to you. Because ultimately, you do not know which student life you could positively impact when you decide to step out of the box and not allow fear to keep you captive.

9

"You Have a Phone Call..."

"The mediocre teacher tells.
The good teacher explains.
The superior teacher demonstrates.
The great teacher inspires."
—WILLIAM WARD

When my classroom video caught the attention of the local news, everybody was in a clamor to get to our school to cover the story. We had to develop necessary procedures in order to make sure my students' learning was not tampered with. My class and I were in the cafeteria eating lunch when I was notified that I had a call at the front office. Immediately I rolled my eyes, agitated at the possibility of being pulled to the front office to take a phone call from a parent during one of the only times teachers have during the day to breathe. As I arrived at the office, my administration and office staff were standing there with stoic expressions on their faces. I asked the school secretary politely, "Who is it?" Ms. Chapman just stared at me and insisted that I take the phone from her, so I did. As I held the phone to my ear, one of the sweetest voices I have ever heard energetically said, "Hello, this is _____ from *The Ellen DeGeneres Show*! How are you today?!" I do not remember my immediate reaction after I heard those words, but somehow, I remained calm. I was more in shock as the conversation continued, but after I hung up the phone, somehow, I was on top of the front office desk, dancing and celebrating. The entire office erupted with cheers and joy. There are not many times we can celebrate something positive happening at our school, and this moment could not have arrived at a better time. For the next two months, I did not hear anything from the show as the school year went on. This was extremely difficult for me because over the two-month span as news circulated around the school and community about the national syndicated show reaching out to our school, trying to keep everybody calm and teach was one of the hardest feats to accomplish.

In December, just before Christmas break, *The Ellen DeGeneres Show* reached out again and said they wanted to come to South Greenville Elementary to record some footage for the EllenTube first-ever teacher series. I quickly agreed without hesitation. I mean, we are talking about Ellen DeGeneres. Only my family knows about this story, but there was a huge snowstorm that hit North Carolina the first week of January, right before my flight was about to leave. I was stuck in my sister's home in Durham due to my car's inability to go up an icy hill. I refused to miss this opportunity. I knew I had worked too hard to get to this point and not go. I packed my bags up, called Uber, and walked 1.5 miles to my destination point to be picked up. I had to reserve a hotel room that Sunday night, but who cared? This was a moment of a lifetime and I rejected the notion to miss this chance to be a pioneer for the project the Ellen DeGeneres team had put together. Little did I know, this was just a ploy to create the surprise of a lifetime. A surprise that I needed to help me reinforce that good things do happen to those who wholeheartedly try their best to do right by others.

To this day, I do not know how Ellen DeGeneres found out about our video. When you compare the analytics and statistical data on the amount of views our original video accumulated, it was nothing short of a miracle. The overwhelming amount of love I have received from people all over the United States, Africa, China, Australia, and other countries confirmed one thing for me. There are still people in this world who understand the value of educators and how we contribute to the overall success of any society. As I read and responded to as many comments as I could, I felt the love and passion through every message. I know some may say that those comments were meant for me, but to be frank, those overwhelming sweet words can apply to all educators around the world. Because unfortunately right now, there are a lot of factors that have negatively impacted the profession of teaching.

Due to the popular opinion of some and the power of social media, the state of education has gained a negative reputation. State laws and federal regulations have constricted the creativity, fluidity, and achievement within the school systems. Some could argue that specific rezoning of school areas has strategically stifled certain demographics and minorities. All across the United States teachers are battling to be compensated adequately, not only for the hours we are at school, but also for the long hours we spend after school to prepare the necessary materials needed to teach our students. Some teachers spend the majority of their weekends completing tasks in order to prepare for the following week. In the midst of educators working this hard, you will find the concrete evidence to who how deep the rivers of strength and perseverance run within a teacher. With so many factors stacked against us, we find a way not only to make things happen, but, to create a world of endless possibilities within our classroom. Each day we face different problems that were not anticipated within the original lesson plans, but yet, we turn unforeseen circumstances into moments of magic in our classrooms. And even as we make the impossible happen daily through our love and instruction, there is often a popular opinion that we *still* are not doing enough. I strongly disagree with that false ideology and I encourage you to believe that not only are you more than enough, your hard work does not go unnoticed. That you are making an impact on your students despite the way they may treat you. You are a catalyst for change in our society.

Teaching is a profession full of superheroes in the flesh. Teachers are not just glorified babysitters, but they are unique beings who have chosen to carry the mantle of building a future for tomorrow. We are individuals who make life-changing decisions every single day in order to ensure the success of our children and schools. This type of hard work is not often highlighted, but there are real problems teachers fight through daily in order to make magic happen. Right now, there is an educator who has a student in his/her classroom who has verbally and physically disrespected them, but every day that teacher must still find a way to try to educate that child. Right now, there is a teacher who has been verbally blasted with harsh curse words and who has unfairly had responsibility placed upon them by an irresponsible parent. But yet, this teacher still wakes up daily to try to find a way to educate students without bias. Across the world, there are educators who teach in school systems that are not properly funded, or forgotten about, or unfairly stereotyped. But these amazing educators find a way to push daily through the political and societal barriers that come with the career of teaching.

I have seen kindergarten teachers with children of their own embrace five-year-olds who do not know their own birthday or how to properly hold a pencil. By their love and hard work, those kindergartners are reading above grade level each year (yes, I am talking about you, Wilson, Baker, Best, Kus, Fields, Pitt, Hartley, and Leneave.) I have seen teachers, despite their salary, take funds to make sure students in their classroom have something adequate to eat or a clean shirt to wear. Or what about educators who have lost important people or relationships while still carrying the responsibilities of an educator? I personally can identify with the weight that brings as you continue to try to make it throughout the day. I did not highlight these specific scenarios as a moment to vent, but to strategically tip my hat to educators all around the world. To bring awareness that we too deal with real-life issues and find ways to teach the geniuses in our classroom. Despite the daily grapple we have with standards and students within our classroom, I see a profession that, for the most part, is full of teachers who are the definition of perseverance and a perfect example for how to maintain excellence when the odds are not in your favor.

When I was at a power luncheon here in Greenville, somebody asked me a question that I was not prepared to answer. They inquired, "Since you have been given a national platform, would you consider yourself to be the face of a positive image for African-American men? The media has often portrayed a negative image of us." I responded to the question to the best of my ability by simply stating how grateful I was for the opportunity and I will gladly assist in helping reframe the many negative images that exist. But as I analyzed the question and the intentions behind it, the more I was able to identify the undeniable reason for the amazing things that have occurred in my life and be blessed for them.

It brings me joy that I have traveled to different countries to experience different cultures, to be fortunate enough to financially bless others without bringing harm to myself, and to provide my students with a unique learning experience. On some days when I am reflecting on my life, I honestly think back to the key individuals who have had a direct impact on my life. And if I were to be forthright with you, the amount of success I have had at twenty-six would not have been possible if it were not for the amazing educators who poured into *my* life. Even though I came from a two-parent household and was never hungry, there were times I made idiotic decisions in school (which is probably why I can relate to some problematic students on a deeper level). I was not the ideal student who loved school and who would be the first student to complain if there were not any homework. But in spite of my opposing behavior to the procedures set forth by my teachers, they found a way to reach me in a remarkable way.

I am a successful positive image for an African-American male because phenomenal educators surrounded me and refused to give up on me. They were relentless in their pursuit to refuse to allow me to become another statistic to a world that has systematically created a school to system pipeline. They rejected the hidden motives by mis-educated individuals to marginalize minorities, but instead they made the conscientious decision to empower me through education. My success that I have now is directly tied to phenomenal, dedicated, and unselfish teachers from eastern North Carolina who wanted to make a difference. Who wanted to see me win, despite my ethnicity or where I come from. When I think about that, it daily reminds me of the power we have as educators. That if we find a way to renew our passion when times get tough within our classroom, we can help change the entire trajectory of a child's future.

To the teacher who is about to quit, who is struggling right now with the specific dynamic of students in their classroom, I have something to say to you. *I understand exactly how you feel.* It is not easy trying to educate the beautiful leaders of tomorrow while simultaneously trying to find a way not to quit your job. The constant challenge to find a way to deal with the turmoil that is happening in your classroom and in your mind is not easy. I personally know how it feels to stay up late at night, dealing with personal issues, only to awaken to the sound of the alarm clock letting you know it is time to go back to your classroom, a place where you do not want to be. At one point for me, I had to apologize to my students because I allowed my failing marriage, random unfortunate circumstances in life, and the unfair advantages of our profession to affect how I treated them. I remember sitting them down in a Socratic circle before our lesson, apologizing to them and promising them I would do better.

I empathize with you and can identify with your frustration in how you are ready to leave the gossiping teachers and disrespectful students behind. *I get it.* After being kicked by another student even after being on *The Ellen DeGeneres Show* (twice), I fully comprehend how you feel. And to be honest, if you choose to leave the teaching profession, I will not blame you nor judge you. You and I both know there are classrooms all across the United States that are full of teachers who do not truly care about the students they face daily. The only reason some of those teachers are still working is to financially stay afloat and for other, laughable, reasons. So if you want to quit, then quit.

But if you want to truly make a difference in a child's life, I encourage you to find a way to fight through the tough seasons. I have learned that as each year passes in our classrooms, we will encounter different students who bring a uniqueness to our everyday life. On some days, things will be wonderful, as every student follows the procedures and is engaged in each lesson. And on others, you may feel that your mind is about to explode if one more student requests to go to the bathroom during your lesson. However your day may go, you must remember the four critical aspects of education that aid in creating a successful classroom climate. It is critical that you identify a reason that will make you unmovable in your classroom, because our students need you.

Before the beginning of my most recent school year, I sat down and made sure I had my four paradigms fully cemented in my educational philosophy. I made sure that I evaluated myself to ensure my passion was authentic and could be felt by every student in my classroom. I researched critical aspects of how to keep proper data to ensure that I was providing students with the appropriate resources for their success. I worked on different ways to relate to the different family dynamics and cultures that walked through my classroom in order to build substantial relationships with my students before instructing them with standards. In addition, I made sure I was prepared with the proper resources to create innovation in my classroom and vowed to always find a way when a student was struggling. But the final icing on the cake would be when I started to analyze the statistical data on the demographic that I served to help me not give up on my babies.

Teaching at a school that is predominantly African-American caused me to dig deeper into the types of barriers they face in the educational system and in our society. One out of four African-American boys are projected to go to prison in their lifetime (see reference number 2). How about the achievement gap that still exists between African-American and minority students versus students of the majority culture, or the percentage of African-American students who are in special education classes? What about the countless studies that have been completed on the disproportionate rate at which African-American students are suspended versus their counterparts? Having knowledge of this data ultimately provided me with the mental understanding and fortitude that hardened my belief to not give up on the profession of teaching. In our classrooms, we have the privilege of helping others defy the low expectations that some individuals in society have systematically and inappropriately placed on students.

As for me, this has been my chance to free others from the *"Trap"* that so many from all walks of life experience. I believe people truly missed the beauty in our original video. Most were excited about the students dancing on tables and how cute they were on camera. But true joy should derive from the fact that students were able to comprehend the text and to answer the questions correctly. They were finally grasping how the power of being able to understand laborious text would afford them more opportunities to further their education. Due to the over-abundance of research on poverty, we know that education can break the power of injustice. What greater privilege is there to help serve a group of young precious kids that some people have already counted out before they reach the final stage of their metamorphosis—even when some of them start with an unfair advantage in life? As this profession becomes tougher to work in, I cannot see myself giving up on my students like so many of their family members and other teachers have done.

I am glad that I did not listen to the many individuals who told me to transfer from South Greenville Elementary, or how "all" of the students are unreachable, or even to my own doubts and fears. If I had allowed the throwing of furniture in my classroom to distract me from my end goal, or the weight of dealing with marital issues while trying to teach destroy me, the priceless life-changing moments that I experienced teaching my babies would have never happened. So with that being said, you must now ask yourself, are you *going to get up or give up?*

References

1. "Come to my office"—Logan Smith. "In North Carolina, Teachers Work Second Jobs to Make Ends Meet," *The Huffington Post*, Dec. 28, 2015. huffingtonpost.com/logan-smith/many-nc-teachers-working_b_8885406.html

2. "You have a phone call"—Glenn Kessler. "The stale statistic that one in three black males 'born today' will end up in jail," *The Washington Post*, June 16, 2015. washingtonpost.com/news/fact-checker/wp/2015/06/16/the-stale-statistic-that-one-in-three-black-males-has-a-chance-of-ending-up-in-jail/?utm_term=.f15652b8c071

Resources

"It takes a village..."

Following is a list of resources that I've found helpful in my teaching career:

Teaching Resources

pbis.org
pbisworld.org
teacherspayteachers.com
masteryconnect.com
classdojo.com
remind.com
kahoot.com
calm.com
khanacademy.com
code.org
educreations.com
ed.ted.com
pbs.org/parents/child-development
pbs.org/education/digitalinnovators

Grants Resources

donorschoose.org
getedfunding.com
teacherscount.org/grants
neafoundation.org/pages/grants-to-educators
adoptaclassroom.org
grantsalert.com
educationworld.com

Reading List

In no particular order, these are books I find inspiring:

Mindset: The New Psychology of Success, by Carol Dweck

Teach Like a Pirate: Increase Student Engagement, Boost Your Creativity, and Transform Your Life as an Educator, by Dave Burgess

The Courage to Teach: Exploring the Inner Landscape of a Teacher's Life, by Parker J. Palmer

The End of Molasses Classes: Getting Our Kids Unstuck—101, Extraordinary Solutions for Parents and Teachers, by Ron Clark

Creating Innovators: The Making of Young People Who Will Change the World, by Tony Wagner

The First Days of School: How to Be an Effective Teacher, 4th Edition, by Harry Wong

The Best Lesson Series: Literature: 15 Master Teachers Share What Works, Edited by Brian Szatbnik

Crash Course: The Life Lessons My Students Taught Me, by Kim Bearden

Teaching with Poverty in Mind, by Eric Jensen

Challenge Questions

For readers who are also teachers—If you think you're ready to "give up," ask yourself these questions:

- When was the last time you visited your student's house?
- What systematic procedures are in place that could potentially harm the trajectory of my students' success?
- Have I addressed any internal problems that are affecting me as a teacher? (Death in the family, past trauma, divorce, and so on.)
- What experiences with other ethnicities has affected your ability to build effective relationships with every student in your classroom?
- What changes can I make within my character that would benefit my students, school, and community?
- When was the last time you offered to help a fellow teacher become a better educator?
- Are your lessons designed to bring cultural awareness, or only classroom content?
- How are you contributing to the school culture and climate? Would your co-workers invite themselves into your classroom to learn something from you?
- Is your grade level team comparing data, collectively working together to build lessons, and consistently communicating about ways to improve student learning? If no, how you change this?
- How are you keeping track of the academic and behavioral data in your classroom?
- When building a lesson for your students, ask yourself, "Would I have fun learning this?"
- How would you describe a dynamic classroom? What could you do to create those qualities in your classroom?
- What have you learned about yourself in the past year? How does that affect you as a teacher?
- Do you hate getting up every day to teach your classroom? What could you change within yourself to fix this situation? If you have changed yourself, what things could you change in your classroom that would help the situation?

A Daily Affirmation

Teaching is the greatest profession in the world,
but every day it does not "feel" like it.
You work day and night to make sure your students have
what they need,
Sometimes at the expense of your own mental, physical,
and emotional health.
Not anymore.
Let me tell you something:
*You are **important** to the world...a necessity.*
You must take care of yourself in order to thrive today.
Your classroom is only as healthy as you are.
*Any negative circumstances and people, simply...**let it go**.*
Yesterday is over, and today is a new day.
Do something in your classroom today that makes you laugh.
Create an unforgettable experience with your students.
*Unapologetically, **have fun** when you are teaching.*
Do not allow today to go by without doing something
*for **yourself** that will make you smile.*
*You are **worth it**.*
*You are **needed**.*
*You are **amazing**.*

Do Not Give Up!